Charles Olson in Connecticut

CHARLES BOER

Charles Olson in Connecticut

with an Introduction by FIELDING DAWSON

NORTH CAROLINA WESLEYAN COLLEGE PRESS

Design by Jonathan Greene

Cover photo: the stone bench next to
the house on Knowlton Hill.

Published by North Carolina Wesleyan College Press,
3400 North Wesleyan Boulevard,
Rocky Mount, North Carolina 27804

Preface

Shortly before he died, in January of 1970, Charles Olson asked that his funeral be an "old-fashioned Irish wake" where his friends would stand around and talk about him. He need not have asked. To those who knew him, "Olson stories" had become something of a genre unto itself, and his "wake" brought out the best of them. It was on this occasion that Allen Ginsberg suggested I write the present account of my own "Olson stories" before, as he put it, "you forget the details and everything turns to mush." Immediately thereafter, I proceeded to write down all the conversations with Olson that I could remember.

While I have tried to fill in the story of Charles Olson's brief visit to Connecticut in 1969 with some additional information about his earlier life, no attempt at all has been made to write a "definitive" biography. In fact, I must caution the reader that what is recorded here is the story of Charles Olson only as he presented himself to me, or to others, at the end of his life; while other sources of information about his biography that I have seen since then would seem to contradict at times Olson's own stories, I have not changed anything in my own account because of these. An example is the story Olson told me of how he learned of the death of President Roosevelt at a poker game in Key West. I have since learned that he was in Washington on that day. These are matters

I happily leave to a full-scale biography to straighten out. In this respect, I hope I am doing what Charles Olson's own model historian, Herodotus, would have done in similar circumstances. Unlike Herodotus, I hasten to add, I haven't made up any of the speeches.

I must acknowledge my debt to the following people, whose memories of Charles Olson, along with my own, make up the substance of this book: Blanche Adams, Charles and Kay Brover, Jack Davis, Oliver Ford, Germaine Girouard, Bernard Horn, Lee Jacobus, Lee Kugler, Paul Kugler, Peter Kugler, John and Glenis Lobb, Thomas and Jean Meddick, William Moynihan, and Mark Zaitchik.

Along with his own stories, John Cech kindly provided me with his notes from Olson's seminar at the University of Connecticut.

Like most people interested in Charles Olson's life and work, I was enormously helped by George Butterick, who made available to me, among other things, an advance copy of his *Annotated Guide to the Maximus Poems of Charles Olson*.

Dr. Peter Gram of the Manchester Memorial Hospital very generously provided a detailed written account of the medical side of the case.

I thank also the Wilbur Cross Library of the University of Connecticut and its staff for allowing me to quote so extensively from previously unpublished work by Charles Olson.

Finally, I must record my thanks to John and Catherine Seelye for their helpful readings of the manuscript. Their counsel and encouragement throughout I despair of acknowledging enough.

C. B.
1975

Introduction

I reread this brilliant work on two successive nights, missing sleep because of an intense wonder: *what would I dream?* But each night at last away I went—into dreamland, waking twice to write them down. I woke on the third morning, however, with a dream I dismissed because I realized I'd read it in Boer's book, and for proof—I recalled—I'd made marginal notes marking the passage. But, sitting at this machine to begin to type, I looked through the book. There were no notes marking the passage. There was nothing at all. Charles Boer had not mentioned it. So my dream was real.

Any work of mystery, and for just that suspense, should be presented with a parallel mystery from a different but kin point of view, so, on page *one* here, I say this book is mysterious because Boer's non-fiction works like Chandler-style fiction.

And as character and background become established, the narrative moves forward along the standard lines of a story, yet from the author's view, in a first and second person singular that enters the final paragraph, and holds, like the true gossamer flow of this work, to the end, without a flaw, or irritant of any kind. That is *something!* Oh *boy!* The suspense operates on a level just under consciousness. You're not aware how you're responding to what you're reading . . . you don't know, in all truth, what you're feeling. It *is* a puzzle, but the author is equal to his subject. The reasons so many writers and other educated, knowledgeable types are terrified of the memoir (anybody can write biography): because the essence of the memoir is its author, and how its subject is seen *by* the author. We see this subject through not only the eyes of the author, but through his ability to confront, and articulate, his responses.

Forbidden in biography! Author STAY OUT! Of course in modern-style biographies, the author has more liberty, but the subject is still the story, the feature, and the point. It may be more flexible, but the biography is of its subject, not its author. Charles Boer's varied narrative is as balanced as a needle afloat, as intricate as a spider's web, for it brings to light aspects of Olson's life and background no other publication has, in that rare combination of a scholar's love for his subject, and comprehension of himself in its context.

But *is* it just for those in the know, that small group of isolated elite who share Boer's impressive range of knowledge, or can a person with a reasonable education not only understand but—the *big* word—*enjoy* it? Yes *if you want to learn*. That's the key.

Because, in this narrow, cramped, mousehole consciousness we live in, and bombarded by censored information, under constant fire at every turn by a barrage of stereotyped characters and rehashed story lines by hacks with word processors, we, even with so little evidence, can sweep all that out of our minds, and begin with what we have, in deference to classical process, begin here at the end, and work back to the beginning. If you want to learn, you've got that itch, you want something fresh, and interesting, your curiosity's up for more than entertainment. (The name of the game, Big Brother's Sister, they're one in the same: he's advertising: she's language: together they work the strings. See the politicians dance?) So to introduce this book to others beside Olson pals and scholars, I'll hint that it works on a few levels, and if you know how to read, it reads as loud and clear between its lines as an umpire's called third strike: *This is history!*

Boer gives Olson's background in politics, which in a throw-away line involves FDR liking Olson. This is true, for at school (Black Mountain) once in a while, not often, Olson spoke in affectionate reverie of Roosevelt . . . and later, of the movie actor John Dierkes (whom I met one day in the late 60's during the cocktail hour, at Max's Kansas City) who had also been in the Office of War Information with Olson—and Ben Shahn . . . and right away, bang! We're involved in American history. Olson's first published book was on Melville (*Call Me Ishmael*) . . . and John Huston wanted Olson to be advisor on *Moby Dick*. Olson went to the West Coast, again encountered Dierkes . . . yes! Acting! In the movie *Shane,* that's Dierkes who gets shot by Alan Ladd, and falls off a platform, head over heels to his death! No stunt man! Well, looking back on it, any study of any kind at all involves in a remarkable way, our history not as seen by Olson, but through him, and in him, his art, his life, as just about everything written on him reveals, one way or another. Pound, and through Pound, T. S. Eliot, as Pound told Olson to send *Ishmael* to Eliot, at Faber & Faber, in London. Eliot turned it down ("Too American") but in 1947, published by Reynal & Hitchcock here, people including De-Kooning, and Eisenstein taken by it . . .

And, which I never knew. Olson doing graduate work at Harvard, Jack Kennedy an undergrad student. Amusing little passage Boer has.

Olson goes every which way including his, and the world of, poetry. History. Scholarship. Boer brilliant keeping hands off the Pound relationship. Also brilliant doing the same, in regards to Olson's wives. Meaning Boer knows his limitations. In his respect for those persons, his humility is classical, even profound. This book is one of those rare ones where what is left out, is in being so, the better.

It is a study in character from one point of view of respect, awe, admiration, the other in, yes, anger, but also irritation, and disagreement delivered with healthy sarcasm. So it isn't a sugar-coated memoir about a legendary poet, and because Boer has a wonderful memory, we are blessed with *pages* of dialogue! Long stretches, with Olson's wit! and Boer no slouch, striking back. Ace-high stuff. Memorable, food for thought. In truth the best. Nothing better has been written by anybody, including me. And Tom Clark, in his informative, sardonic biography.

The other vital books, very few, are *Olson & Pound,* by Olson, edited (invaluable) by Catherine Seelye, and of course—perhaps a secret document—Olson's own memoir, *Post Office,* of his father, with a memoir of a friend of the Olson family, Mr. Meyer, and the one and only short story, "Stocking Cap." These brief works form Olson's creative/poetic DNA, are a little mind-boggling in how revealing they are . . . most unusual. From these works, plus of course Olson's writing (in particular, *The Mayan Letters,* and—*Maximus Poems* without saying—but the two books of his shorter poems, the latter more revealing—*Collected Poems,* and *A Nation of Nothing but Poetry.*)

There are no qualifications in my admiration for Boer's book. No apologies for little errors here and there, or as critics write: *but, in spite, it's still a fine book. No qualifications, none* of that. This book is a direct encounter with a vivid 20th century man and poet who has been misunderstood only because of bored, unimaginative, in fact resentful and jealous know-it-alls who have NOT done their field work. It should also be said, fuck the fair shake people. Olson was not involved in fair shakes, and for one real reason, which this book in its most artistic and impressive way points to:

Olson was deceptive in his personality and, therefore, his work was written to hide, to conceal—as was all work about him, including this book and this *Introduction.* He was a mystery also because he *loved* a mystery, and in that way, this all said, however . . . he *was* complete and like Mozart who never finished his *Requiem* because it was in everything he wrote. Period. Olson would have continued writing, meaning his work would continue to change, in no way becoming more clear, as in all our efforts to get what we want in there, and make it clear.

No.

Olson's task was to write what he wanted so he could leave the rest out. His deception was we would believe it, just as we do. We should. There, after all, it is, isn't it? Yes. But just as it is there it is also not there. Olson's selection of an subject anywhere, anyhow, pivots on how much he can say and leave unsaid.

He returned to Gloucester in his epic *Maximus* in his secret, still childish fear of childhood. Olson's childhood, again like Mozart, tells a *lot,* and Boer's wise, cool, masterful hints can serve as doors flung wide open, for further study. The so little we have is, in the knowledge the poet would keep it hidden, in an increasing modern truth, enough. For no matter which way the question is turned, in his own poem, what was buried behind Lufkin's diner, in Gloucester, was, no matter as Boer recounts, *even as Olson told Boer it came in a dream,* of "lovekin" . . . "two children had been murdered and buried there." So typical of Olson to satisfy Boer by baffling him, it in part becomes the very style of this book, as it's a memoir, Olson dies, at the beginning of a section regarding Thanksgiving, Olson's favorite holiday, 1969, November what, 24th? we know he died first week Jan., 1970, what is going on? In an almost throwaway line, Boer writes (you) "complained about a soreness in your ear that was keeping you awake."

So, I thought.

As in the best of Raymond Chandler an unconscious focus swerves onto the author, for he will be the one who will tell us what will happen. Olson thereby takes one step into his background, and the author spins out the rest, needle still afloat, he spins his web, with omissions as his silent orchestra.

Between the lines of Olson's telling him his dream, of the two murdered children, the "lovekin" buried behind the diner, Olson didn't say who they were. Perfect.

"Your own interest in the theory of your cancer was extraordinary. You told the doctors that you thought it had all started in your throat. They said that was impossible. It could only start that way in women. At this you became very excited. 'Follow that up!' you said. 'Because I *am* more woman than man. The woman is the creative part of me. All artists are part woman.'"

The grasp of Olson's myth is, therefore, complete, and Boer's synopsis of the meaning of Olson's work is stunning. Never to be forgotten, as well, are their exchanges of wit, and humor. Often subtle, deft. Warm. Not a man afraid to love—neither of 'em.

I stood before a wall, as at the Mayan ruin by the side of the road, where we stopped, got out and gazed upon it . . . but instead of stones, they were pages of books, peeling, corners worn, waterstained, turning brown, and cracked, wrinkled . . .

A letter, a page from a manuscript, and was there also an envelope? Yes. With stamp cancellation, but blurred, date unclear, with the faded address and paper worn, and soft, in my hands.

In the third dream a page from Boer's book appeared, the passage where he writes that Olson had to learn how to read his work, and that he (Olson) had thanked a certain person unknown to me, who had taught him. But it was a marked-up manuscript page, in typescript, many notations and re-writes, in several voices quibbling, page came closer blurring it, the edges curled as if over heat, and it became, in its rough, misshapen form, like a stone, and before me, fit into its place.

So at my typewriter yesterday, June 11, 1990 before I began this Introduction, I checked through Boer's book for that passage, where, I knew, I had made a note in the margin, agreeing with Boer, for Olson had, in 1950 and '51, in reading aloud, not read the words as they were written, but as if they were written in sentences and phrases ("Issue, Mood"), and not being able to remember who it was whom Olson had thanked for teaching him how to read, I gave Boer's pages close scrutiny, but it—none of it—was there, anywhere, in the book. So. I had dreamed that, too.

Olson had been my teacher at Black Mountain, and had from Yucatan written me. Also—earlier—from D.C. I wrote him, as well. Allow me to say that I appear as another one of his students, from Black Mountain days, and that is true. But it was more than that—no, it was different. We say it was the politician in him that knew how to deal with a variety of people, and that's true, but it was also in his character to be secretive, as it was with Franz Kline, who said different things to different people. Olson too, in that way, and after he had arrived at Boer's house, early in the book, they go out for a walk, the ultra mystical event in this text takes place: Olson, just arrived in Connecticut . . . Boer:

"You would turn to me, hold your face about an inch from mine, which made me nervous, and demand to know if I was not in fact an angel sent to guide you through paradise. You insisted that I tell you the truth!

"I knew you had been studying the angelology of Ibn Arabi, the thirteenth-century Arab theologian and mystic, but . . . as far as I knew, I wasn't an angel to (do that), or . . . didn't think I was.

" 'Are you absolutely sure?' You asked . . ."

Later that day Olson gave Boer a stone that, without Boer's knowing it, he had picked up during their walk. It is, Olson said, ". . . the nicest thing I have to give you." And that night Olson wrote a poem, re Knowlton's Hill, in his style, and Boer remarks that, "In only one day the land was yours."

True.

This was, it seems to me, clear, although not a word, a syllable the most subtle hint (save in desperate emotion), of Olson's motive for the visit which was not a visit, but a planned exit. I think Olson in Gloucester, where he returned from teaching in Buffalo in 1965, after his wife Betty's death, a couple of years of spirit-isolate living brought him in spite of his studies and art, little but the gulf of his past, and it could be because *this is how it happens,* and he follows his father's footsteps, in *just* this kind of impulse: to get out. I think on top of it he knew he was going to die, conscious knowledge or not, in most part not, but he knew. Cancer of the liver doesn't show up like a sudden shot, there are early signals which he, typical, wouldn't let anyone know. And part of the reason he was so irrational and violent was, he didn't have Connie or Betty (more mothers) around to tell him to cool it, so to himself he was free to talk, and bully, even threaten Boer.

Read the reason Olson chose Boer to visit, it's right there, between the lines. Olson had selected him.

The man who had declared SPACE to be central fact in 1947, had given it up, and become a temporal man like everybody else because like everybody else, he was dying. And, on those lines, he was in his eleventh hour. Yet of course the genius, the magic, skill, discipline and vision abounded as he kept track, and in another poem, near the end—note the reference to Lufkin—written on a napkin:

> "I live underneath
> the light of day
> I am a stone,
> or the ground beneath
>
> My life is buried,
> with all sorts of passages . . ."

These cross-references form his work and life.

And look at *this!* Not a dream after all! Page 55, I just found it! Olson had not at school read his poems according to his line breaks, and just as my notes in the margin indicate: *not the way the line breaks worked.* Beside the paragraph where Olson thanks David Tudor, "a very knowing pianist" indeed! for telling him to read "what's written on the page." *Not* what Olson would *make* of them!

Not a dream after all. So.

I could write a book about this book, and if I did I'd give detail to Boer's direct, handsome, and moving accuracy on the limitations of Olson and *Maximus*. Page 112 is a lesson for us all or . . . for me for sure. "Every line is a celebration of this man in his history, in his city, in his self. But they are, alas, celebrations for an elite. . . ."

Boer quotes a stanza, to illustrate, but since 1975 when this book was published, not too long after Olson's death, our society and the planet have changed much for the worse. We have regressed to images of material happy-things, in a many-millioned loss of identity on a dying earth with but one guarantee: *no* safety. The fires still burn in Kuwait.

> Polis now
> is a few, is a coherence not even yet new (the island
> of this city is a mainland now of who? who can say who are
> citizens?

Good question!

Olson may have intended an elite few, but his words go beyond his meaning and intent. In this he mapped out the way we can write our lives, adding background just as he did, galaxies of proper nouns—names of the people in *our* lives: what they were, where they lived, the lanes, the streets, the avenues, buildings, empty lots, woods, rivers—cemeteries, too, write of our families and relatives and neighbors, friends, enemies, alive or—not! Even from the grave, like Olson did, and like he did not: we can write what he avoided: to the last three words of this book. what he did not *do* but pointed *to:* dare to tear our hearts out, and blind with grief and love, hammer it home on paper: burn alive in our poetry nay *every* poem nay *all* art, in the future, what each of us is who we are, where we come from so others *all* the others will know, and on that foundation, begin to reshape, redefine, and renew our planet, and ourselves in one.

This is what we can make of Charles Olson's mystery and myth, deceptions and many exits, which characterized his life and art, for reasons which go unwritten here because they don't belong here. This book is just what it should be: a perception of the Master, by his chosen, former student, Charles Boer. It's different than the one you will write, and different from mine, as well. Never more than what it is. In hand. Complete.

FIELDING DAWSON
May 13, 1991
New York City

Charles Olson in Connecticut

"Cholly, how are ya?"

It was your best campaign voice, your hurry-it-up telephone voice suddenly booming in my ear. You always made it sound like the telephone had just been invented and might give out at any minute.

"I'm fine, Charles," I said. "How are you?"

"Well, I'm okay, I mean I'm all right. I'm on the road, or at least the railroad. I'm at the train station in Gloucester taking a vacation, and I was wondering how it would be if I came down to pay you a visit?"

I was delighted. I had invited you to Connecticut many times, but it was like inviting the Pope. I never really expected you to come. It was a rare day anymore when Charles Olson was willing to leave Gloucester.

Only a few weeks before, on my way back from a trip to Newfoundland, I stopped off at your apartment. When I walked up the back steps you were sitting on the porch reading a postcard I had sent, which by some coincidence had just arrived. The postcard said that I was on an expedition in search of Viking ruins, and wouldn't come back without some.

"Well, don't look at *me*," you said in greeting.

You had yourself just returned from a short visit to Maine with your daughter. That trip had only confirmed your reluctance to travel, you said. You were happy the summer was over, happy that Gloucester would soon lose its summer crowds and return to its ordinary hard business as a fishing port. With the tourist season behind it for another year, Gloucester's restaurants, a little richer, would be Olson's again. Its news, via *The Gloucester Times,* would supply serious daily reading once more. Its streets would again be your merciless talking-ground. The poet of Gloucester could get back to work.

Or so it seemed then. Now, suddenly, you had changed your mind and wanted out. I was too excited by the prospect of your coming to ask why.

I immediately offered to drive up to get you, a distance of a hundred miles. But you insisted on coming by train. You loved trains. Unfortunately, there was no train to Mansfield, Connecticut. There had not been one in years. The nearest train station was in Hartford, twenty-five miles to the west.

"No train?" you said, as if astounded by the news, your enthusiasm for the whole venture appearing to fade.

I assured you that I could drive to Gloucester in no time, but your heart was absolutely set on a train ride. I got the impression in fact that you had gone to the train station before you even knew where you wanted to go. You decided to take the train as far as Boston, where I would meet you with my car.

You started naming restaurants there where we could meet, but most of those you named had closed years ago, and you had never heard of the ones I named. We finally settled on that old Teutonic stand-by, the Wursthaus in Harvard Square.

It was Friday, September 26, 1969. It took me an hour and a half to drive from Mansfield to Cambridge, and it should have taken you only half an hour on the train from Gloucester. But I arrived at the restaurant first and was waiting for you outside for at least another half hour. I began to wonder if you had changed your mind, if you had found a more interesting train to somewhere

---

4

else, if you had got on a Pullman perhaps and were now comfortably asleep in Rhode Island.

And then you appeared, bobbing leisurely up the street, always slower than anyone else by at least half. You walked slowly because of your size, all six feet eight inches of it, and because Charles Olson was one man who would never be rushed. Dressed in old corduroys and work boots, a heavy winter overcoat over a sweater, your winter cap perched loosely on top with its flap dropping over the ears, you seemed ready for the Arctic Circle, not this warm fall afternoon in Cambridge. And you were smiling, laughing even, all the way up the street once you spotted me waving to you. You looked great.

We went into the restaurant and ordered bratwurst and beer. With an affectionate grasp of the waitress's wrist, you insisted that it be "a good piece of meat, dear!"

She was amused. This was Olson, the teaser of waitresses, a role I had seen you play many times. When the bratwurst came, you took one bite and abandoned it. When the waitress came back and saw that you hadn't eaten it, she became very solicitous, and asked if you wanted her to take it back for something else. You indulged her solicitude for all it was worth, but wouldn't send the bratwurst back.

You told me how excited you were to be on the move again, but lost no time in directing the conversation toward the latest news in archaeology and the latest books about the Second Millennium B.C. You were kept up-to-date on developments in the archaeology of the Near East through that odd network of friends and contacts you had in this country and in England—the Olson mafia. These people sent you any information they came upon, no matter how trivial. You read it all, and thanked them profusely.

The Second Millennium was one of your great subjects. Our time, you used to say, was nothing more than a return to it. Never mind the future-shockers, the media analysts, the apocalypse people, America was returning—or should be returning, you thought—to a condition of mind that prevailed in the pre-Socratic mythlands of ancient Crete and Asia Minor. And no Olson conversation got very far before discussing the most recent work of such scholars as Samuel Noah Kramer on Sumer, Cyrus Gordon on Ugarit, James Mellaart on Anatolia, or G. L. Huxley on the Luvians.

Your ability to refer to the history and archaeology of these lands was as expert and detailed as any field worker's, although few field workers in archaeology would have the imagination, or the wit, to apply it all so broadly to a sense of the present.

You had considered yourself a serious mythologist for at least twenty years. You said the original impetus to study such remote material came to you after reading the Foreword to D. H. Lawrence's *Fantasia of the Unconscious*. You were quick to add that, as a whole, you considered Lawrence's book atrocious, but the Foreword was well worth reading. And indeed it is, especially in terms of understanding your own esoteric prose of the Fifties and Sixties.

Behind Lawrence's disclaiming tone in the Foreword, there is a striking Olsonian lift and sweep to it all. Even the first hammering of what you call "the hinges of civilization to be put back on the door," in your *Proprioception* pamphlet, can be heard in the prose of Lawrence's own mythological construction company. With magnificent abandon, Lawrence envisioned an omniscient Atlantis civilization drowned by the melting of the glaciers and a world flood, followed by a great dispersal of "refugees from the drowned continents" moving to "the high places of the world," where "some degenerated naturally into cave men" and "some retained their marvelous innate beauty and life-perfection, as the South Sea Islanders." These refugees nonetheless maintained what Lawrence called "the old wisdom, only in its half-forgotten, symbolic forms . . . remembered as ritual, gesture, and myth story."

6

Here, too, were the seeds of your famed "Human Universe" essay, its pleasure in rediscovering the Mayans' lost knowledge of the body, their ease of touch, the prelogical sense of life, all grafted from Lawrence's fantastic garden where the great myths "now begin to hypnotize us again, our own impulse towards our own scientific way of understanding being almost spent."

In February of 1951, having obtained a grant for archaeological study, you went to Lerma on the Yucatan Peninsula. You stayed for several months, studying the ruins of Mayan civilization, "the old wisdom," their "cosmic graphs." As the historian of Gloucester who would liken himself to Herodotus, as the poet of *The Distances*, the "archaeologist of morning," how you must have swooned when you first read Lawrence's lines about "the wide world of centuries and vast ages—mammoth worlds beyond our day, and mankind so wonderful in his distances, his history that has no beginning yet always the pomp and the magnificence of human splendour unfolding through the earth's changing periods."

"The trouble with professors today," I heard you exclaim, so often and so painfully, "is that they don't *believe* what they know."

It was Lawrence's exclamation too. "Our vision, our belief, our metaphysic is wearing woefully thin, and the art is wearing absolutely threadbare," he wrote. "We have no future; neither for our hopes, nor our aims, nor our art. It has all gone grey and opaque. We've got to rip the veil of the old vision across, and find what the heart really believes in, after all: and what the heart really wants, for the next future. And we've got to put it down in terms of belief and knowledge. And then go forward again, to the fulfillment in life and art."

It's striking, for the reader of Charles Olson, to read Lawrence's public-baiting, critic-baiting, elitist remarks in this anomalous book on what he thought was "the new psychology." It is a book not addressed to "the generality of readers," hoping instead to "thin their numbers considerably" by its aim at "the solar plexus."

For thinned as their numbers undoubtedly were, Lawrence had here attracted, in you, Charles, someone who would sense the value of "ritual, gesture, and myth-story" more profoundly than he could have dreamed.

After all, the author of *Fantasia of the Unconscious* had to disclaim any expertise in scholarship. "It is not for me to arrange fossils, and decipher hieroglyphic phrases," he said. He preferred to go only with "hints" from what he called "dead wisdom."

You, on the other hand, would take it all on, cowed by no man's specialization. It is no exaggeration to say that you made yourself more conversant with the languages of the Near East, with Anatolian artifacts and Mayan hieroglyphics, with the Deglaciation and other "mammoth worlds beyond our day" than any other so-called layman. Such study, you once wrote, was a duty for you, because "otherwise the present will lose what America is the inheritor of: a secularization which not only loses nothing of the divine but by seeing process in reality redeems all idealism from theocracy or mobocracy, whether it is rational or superstitious, whether it is democratic or socialism."

The price for such erudite forays, of course, would be to turn off as many readers as you would attract. You became "controversial," aggravating a literati that typically questioned the propriety of all this bizarre stuff as a ground for "modern poetry." Your reply was to declare yourself "post-modern," no idle pronouncement for one who tried so hard to do what Lawrence had so easily proposed—"Rip the veil of the old vision across, and walk through the rent."

Your first question to me that afternoon in the Wursthaus was a familiar one. "You got anything for me?"

I had very little, as you must have known, because you had read everything—and what interest I had in the myth and history of this era was caught from you in the first place when I was your student several years before.

I had been trained as a classicist when I first met you, and my own attitude toward your Second Millennium utopia was the conservative academic scepticism that is obligatory for all card-carrying classicists. There is nothing new in our old subject, I re-assured myself, that hasn't already been pointed out by some dead German. Better be careful, I thought, when listening to the extravagant and unheard of claims for the wonders of prehistoric man being made by this *poet* who couldn't even read *Greek!* I was so steadfast a nonbeliever, in fact, that I once let you bet me five-hundred dollars that in five years the dates for certain mythological events on an archaic Greek inscription called "The Paros Chronicle" would be proven correct by scholars

"You can't give a date for the birth of Aphrodite!" I argued like a fool.

By 1968, however, when the bet fell due, you had me convinced, not so much by "The Paros Chronicle" perhaps as by the force and grace of your imagination alone. Who could have known?

Most of our Wursthaus conversation that September afternoon was about James Mavor's new book, *Voyage to Atlantis*. You were thrilled by it because it set out to prove scientifically, with ocean-ographic experiment, something that had always been considered, except by quacks, a mythological question—the historical existence of Plato's Atlantis. And Mavor dated its sinking to the middle of the Second Millennium B.C.—Olson territory!

As a mere oceanographer, Mavor had been subject throughout his work to an overbearing surveillance on the part of the official Greek archaeologist at the site, Dr. Spyridon Marinatos. You told me, in a conspiratorial tone of voice reflective of the book itself, that you had just finished telephoning Mavor at the Woods Hold

Oceanographic Institute to ask him further questions about the discovery, but also to tell him "not to let that Marinatos marinate you any further!"

We left the restaurant after a couple of hours and decided to take a walk through Harvard Yard, where we had both spent some time, many years apart, as graduate students. Crossing the street to enter it, you were especially rankled by the new buildings. They all looked like business offices, you said, and all painted in pastel television colors.

"What's happened to the place?" you asked. "Well, it just goes to show you."

The first building we came to inside Harvard Yard was Boylston Hall, west of the Classics Department. I pointed out to you that this was the home of Eric Havelock, whose book, *Preface to Plato,* you admired very much. Havelock was one of your few academic heroes.

Havelock had been one of my teachers, and I recommended his book to you when we first met. I never heard the end of it for the three years I studied with you. *Preface to Plato* became *the* text in your seminars. Students used to borrow your copy from week to week, since no one ever thought to buy it, figuring you'd soon get off the subject and on to something else. You never did. We even read it in class while you talked. Every so often you had to call out for it, "Havelock, Havelock, who's got the Havelock?"

As we approached the steps of Boylston Hall, another of my old instructors was coming out, a man I disliked very much. I wasn't keen on talking to him, or even saying hello. I nudged you to move along, telling you that I couldn't bear to encounter the man again. But you were as always very slow to move or be moved, and you started pushing me back, with increased amusement, saying, "Don't be afraid of those guys."

I told you it was not a matter of fear but of preference, and I implored you to keep on walking. You were grinning now and started pushing me back to the steps. Only at the last insufferable second did you yield and move on.

"Yeah, I know what you mean," you said. "They scare me too."

Charles Olson goes to Harvard as a graduate student in 1936. It is not the happiest time for him either. By the spring of 1939, he completes the coursework for a Ph.D. in that new subject, "American Civilization," though he never writes a dissertation and thus never receives the degree.

It is a critical period in his life, when, at age 29, he envisions himself as headed for an academic career. At Harvard he takes a course with Frederick Merk in "The Westward Movement." This course will have a lasting effect on his later work. He studies Melville with F. O. Matthiessen, writing a paper for him that he later publishes as "Lear and Moby Dick." He does the spadework for his celebrated study of Melville, *Call Me Ishmael,* tracking down a number of important volumes of Melville's personal library. No one but Olson, who scribbles information endlessly in his own books, would think of such a project.

He meets Edward Dahlberg as well in that summer of 1936. The two could not be more remarkable in contrast. Dahlberg, a lonely scourge of American letters, is contemptuous of all writing and writers since the seventeenth century. A genius of jeremiads, Dahlberg tries to educate Olson in the sorrowful ways of the soul. It is a shaky friendship from the first, and one that ends bitterly—but not before Dahlberg is successful in opening a creative vein in Olson.

In the summer of 1938, Olson begins his own "westward movement," hitchhiking to San Francisco for the first time. He returns to Harvard in the fall of 1938, exhausted and tense, unable to revise "Lear and Moby Dick" for publication in Dorothy Norman's magazine *Twice-a-Year*—his mother still considerably upset and on hard times three years after his father's death; and, as if that is not enough, he finds himself evicted from his room at Harvard's John Winthrop House, the next tenant having dumped all his worldly belongings into a little pile outside the door. Harvard!

By the following spring his nerves give way altogether and he enters a hospital in Boston for a rest. He leaves Harvard for good, aided by a Guggenheim grant for his Melville work, and spends the rest of the year living with his mother in Gloucester. From this experience will come his first poems, and an essay on myth. The life of an academician is not for Olson.

Thirty years later you were taking another look at the place. The intervening time had not raised it in your esteem.

We walked by some student residence halls which I pointed out to you had once been occupied by George Washington's troops during the Revolutionary War.

"I never knew that," you said, "but I'm glad to hear it, because let me tell you, that's where revolutionaries belong!"

We strolled back to my car. I groaned when I saw a parking ticket on the windshield.

"Don't pay it," you said, rather too freely. "They'll never know. I never pay."

It was too reminiscent of the advice you always handed out to young writers, aspiring revolutionaries, and inquiring rough-necks: "Go to jail. You've got to go to jail sometime if you're going to be any good."

You said you were relieved my car as a Peugeot and "not one of those little things," meaning a Volkswagen. You hated Volkswagens, primarily because you were simply too big to squeeze into them. But there was another reason too.

It was in a Volkswagen that your wife, Betty, had been killed only five years before in a tragic accident in Buffalo. She had gone out one wintry afternoon to buy groceries. Her car was hit by a drunken driver in a head-on collision. When the State Police appeared at the door to tell you of the accident, you collapsed. Your life was suddenly, incredibly, broken apart. You would never be able to put it back together again.

You had apparently forgotten that I bought my car after you had warned me once, turning pale as you spoke, "Whatever you buy, *do not buy a Volkswagen.*"

It was not advice. It was an ultimatum. And for once I did what you told me.

We drove back to Connecticut over the Massachusetts Turnpike. The scenery seemed to refresh you. That there still existed such vast uninhabited areas of forest in New England came as something of a surprise to you. Nonetheless, you were for buying it all up. There was an urgent need to buy land these days, you argued.

"Look at what's-his-name, that Arlo Guthrie, buying all that land in Vermont." You wanted to do the same. Your term for this was "the new tycoonery," and you started naming all the people you thought were engaging in it. It was "the new capitalism," you said, though it sounded to me very much like the old capitalism. The only requirements were that one be alive and have a lot of money.

When we arrived at my house in Mansfield you became excited. The house was majestically set on top of a great hill overlooking miles of Connecticut woodlands and valleys. It was built by a retired sea captain, who imitated the large houses by the sea in Newport and New London with their sprawling porches and turrets. In your excitement as we drove up the long circular driveway you started accusing *me* of "the new tycoonery" for having such a place, though I only rented. All of a sudden you wanted to know why I had never invited you here before. But I had, many times, and you knew it.

I finally asked why you had decided to come down for a visit now, why you felt like leaving Gloucester when only a few weeks earlier you had seemed so settled there.

"I hate Gloucester," you said. "I *abhor* Gloucester!"

It was a strange admission, I thought, for the author of *The Maximus Poems*—that monumental celebration of Gloucester's history and people that you had spent nearly twenty years in writing.

Nonetheless, on a later occasion, one of my students was talking with you about Gloucester and referred to it enthusiastically as "Root City," your own term for it in *The Maximus Poems*.

You immediately, and rather angrily, replied in your most gravelly voice, "I don't have any roots in that city!"

Your feelings were always mixed on the subject. It was a love/hate relationship, with hate presently in the ascendant.

Once you told us of a murder that had just been committed in Gloucester. You told the story in hushed, dramatic tones; how a man whom you knew rather well had killed his wife and cut her up with a butcher knife. The police weren't certain yet that the husband was the murderer, and hadn't arrested him. But you knew. You described how you sat in a restaurant looking at the murderer through a bunch of potted plants, when suddenly. . . . But then I started laughing so much at this demonstration of Olson the private eye, at your gesture in pushing back the plants to see, that unfortunately my laughter ended the story. It was so much like Zero Mostel playing Sam Spade.

But how struck you were by the fact that you knew this murderer personally—the first actual murderer you had ever known. Murder was always in the family, you said. It was a family affair. "And this is where it was happening, this murder. And you know you're always trying in life to get close to the center, where everything's happening—well, this was it, the center, and I was there. And the problem today of why people are so off-center is because they're so off family."

Yet for you, Charles, merely to be off Gloucester was to be off-center. Charles Olson had come to Mansfield.

We had a long and leisurely supper that first night, though again you seemed to eat very little. I attributed this to my cooking—you were a stickler for good food and liked nothing more than to spend entire evenings at the dinner table. The only sign of the old Olson appetite this night, however, was the speed with which you drank a dozen cups of coffee.

Afterwards, like the scrupulously polite guest that you were at first, you insisted that I continue to do everything that I would do if you weren't there.

"You don't really mean that," I said, "because if you do, it means we watch the movie on television."

"The movie it is then," you said, "because yes, I do mean it." You emphasized that you were ready to do whatever I did, with pleasure.

Two of my best friends, Peter and Paul Kugler, who were students at the University of Connecticut, called up, and I invited them over to meet you. They brought several bags of sandwiches to eat during the movie. The sandwiches were for them, but they'd heard of the famous Olson appetite, and thoughtfully included a half-dozen extras for you. I don't think they really expected you to eat that many, but they weren't taking any chances. Nonetheless, you ate them all, as if to oblige, though you couldn't have been that hungry.

The Kuglers were excited—even a little stunned—to be watching television with the great Charles Olson, whose work they had studied in my poetry course.

15

And you were happy to meet them. The three of you horsed around for awhile, even arm-wrestled while waiting for the movie to start. You told them how you too had played soccer once, on the Wesleyan team, which, like a good alumnus, you asked them about, since the University of Connecticut often played Wesleyan. You said you had played goalie, and then started demonstrating for them by blocking their imaginary shots to your imaginary net in the living room. They were impressed.

At one point, when you wanted more coffee, you grabbed my arm as I was going to the kitchen, and playfully started twisting it, while telling me how much sugar you wanted. I pretended to wince in pain, since I didn't want to be the only straight-man in the room. Peter, as he saw me wince, immediately jumped up to rescue me from what I pretended was excruciating pain. You laughed, Olson, at his credulity, and then told me I had good reliable friends. You were in a happy mood.

We settled down to the movie, *The Brothers Karamazov*. It didn't take you long to become immersed in it. You watched as intensely as if it were live theater, and when each commercial break came, you would immediately begin to expound to us on the quality of the acting, the plot, the particular brilliance of Dostoevsky. Though I had made a fire in the fireplace, you wrapped yourself up in a blanket, and sat there yourself looking like some grand Russian patriarch in the robes of office. You loved the movie, and demanded "more movies about old novels."

You turned to the Kugler brothers suddenly and asked, "What do *you* think about it? What does *your* generation think about a movie like this?"

They were struck by the seriousness with which you watched television, and could only say that they liked it too.

Charles Olson is a long-standing film buff. In 1938, as a member of the Harvard Film Society, Olson gets up before the audience when his favorites (especially Eisenstein) are shown, and introduces each film with a little commentary. One of his friends and fellow students, Leonard Bernstein, plays the piano in the little theater where the films are shown as people come in to take their seats. Then, if the film is not a talky, Bernstein plays background music as the reels unroll.

While we were watching *The Brothers Karamazov*, there was a knock at my door. It was another student, Tom Meddick, who lived across the street. His wife was sick, he said, and he didn't know what to do. (He had only been married a month.) Should he call a doctor? Should he take her to the hospital right away? After getting all the particulars of the case, I recommended calling a doctor for advice.

You listened to this exchange, Charles, with one ear on *The Brothers Karamazov* and one ear on Meddick. Finally you got up, towering over him, and said, "Go on home and take care of her, for Christ's sake. What are you doing over here? Your wife's all right, she just needs *you!*"

After he left, you turned to me and asked, almost angrily, "Why doesn't he take care of his own medical business? Why does he come to you?"

That first night in Mansfield you slept in the guest room, putting the mattress of one bed on top of the other so that you would be high enough for your extraordinary length not to be restricted by the footboard of an average man's bed.

Over the bed hung a painting. It was my own attempt to copy a larger painting by Franz Kline, my favorite painter. I had forgotten that Kline was a friend of yours. Had I known you were coming, I certainly would have taken it down. When you saw it, you burst out laughing.

"Well, it just goes to show you," you said, "there's only one Franz Kline."

"I know," I said.

You paused a moment, then added, "But Franz would have loved you. In fact, you remind me of him."

That night, and for many nights to come, you took large amounts of the refrigerator's contents to bed with you—everything from a jug of orange juice, a quart of ginger ale, candy, a head of lettuce to a box of crackers, cheese and hard-boiled eggs. Your arms loaded, you staggered back into the room and dumped everything on the bed.

You also wanted things to read in bed, and I regularly offered you a book or two that I thought you might not have read. Among other things, you agreed to read *Land to the West* by Geoffrey Ashe, a book on the weather conditions in antiquity by Rhys Carpenter, and an illustrated book called *Secret Societies*. The books had to be informational, no novels and certainly no poetry; and the information had to be of such a kind that the man who wrote it used himself somewhere in the book, drawing out of his own person the theory of the book.

Nonetheless, every time I gave you such a book you were sceptical and reluctant to take it, though the next day (you would get up in the early afternoon of the next day) you would be terribly excited about the previous night's reading, with notes and plans to pursue the book. It would start all over again the next night with the same scepticism and reluctance about the next book. You were a hard man to please.

I remember well that first night, after you had finally gone to bed (the whole ritual could take hours), hearing you in the next room furiously turning the pages of the books, munching vigorously on the lettuce and other food. Every few hours that night I was suddenly awakened by a new burst of frantic munching and page-turning. It went on all night.

The next day, Saturday, was unusually balmy, the trees had started turning, and the view from the back windows of the house, over the hillside, was magnificent. The most glorious of all seasons on earth, fall in New England, was beginning.

You sat in the window seat, coffee in hand, and stared out at birds and squirrels romping on the hill and in the distance. Suddenly you decided to take a walk. I offered to guide you on a tour of the hills and woods, and we set out at about two in the afternoon.

When we got outside, you decided that you didn't need the heavy winter coat you had put on, so you dropped the coat on the ground at the top of the hill behind the house. (Once, on an equally balmy night in Gloucester, going out to dinner, I asked you why you were wrapping yourself up in so many layers of heavy clothes, and you replied, "Because you never know when you're coming back!")

We started down into the woods and soon came to a clearing where there were some large rocks underneath two enormous and ancient oak trees. I told you the place reminded me of Dodona, the oracular shrine of Zeus in Greece that is famous for its oaks; so you, all seriousness, suggested that we sit in silence and listen. We sat there, with you respectful and observant of every chipmunk and squirrel that moved warily near us, when suddenly we heard the Kugler brothers coming down the path in the woods.

"Be quiet and maybe they won't see us," you said, apparently wanting nothing more now than privacy and the pleasure of nature. I couldn't figure out how they had guessed we were down here, but you could.

"It's me again," you said. "They're good scouts, good Indians, and it was just dumb old me leaving a trail a mile long with my coat back there."

When they found us, you asked them to go ahead down the path and scout a trail for us "like good Indians." They went a little farther and then decided it was best to leave. I was disappointed in you, but I said nothing. It made me uneasy to see you reject people so abruptly, when only the night before you were so friendly.

We continued the walk down to the bank of a spring-fed lake at the bottom of the hill. There were no houses or any sign of people, and you sat down, marveling at the stillness of the lake.

"This is paradise," you said, obviously enraptured by the place as you stared at the afternoon sun on an expanse of water lilies or at an occasional frog that would make its precipitous move from a near rock. You said it was "the earth as it should have stayed."

While I agreed, I told you I was afraid that someday it would all be ruined by land speculators and developers.

"No," you said, "this is paradise, and don't worry about that sort of thing. All that matters is that it's here now, and we're here now too. I didn't even know this place existed last week. Don't ever worry about anything."

We sat at the lake bank for about half an hour. You talked enchantingly about the shape of the earth. How sensitive you were to the slightest shift in a landscape. You would notice the most minute variations in soils or rocks or vegetation.

We moved on into more woods. You handled it all well, which surprised me—even a barbed wire fence that you crawled under with ease despite your size.

Since our conversation had already taken a mythological turn, you started talking about your work on myth, especially *Causal Mythology*, which had just been published that summer. You said you regretted that you never seemed to get down on paper what you really wanted to say on the subject. A few weeks before this, however, when you presented me with a copy of the book, you said it represented your best statement on myth. Now you spoke of the possibility of our doing a myth book together, where I would ask you specific questions that I was interested in, and you would answer at leisure, instead of your usual approach—a lecture, where you had to answer random audience questions on the spot. While nothing further came of this idea, we continued to talk of it then.

There were only three proper areas for the study of myth, you said: *initiatic cosmos, the world of nature,* and *the celestial world.* And you kept repeating them throughout the walk, as places or incidents would suggest them. I had to ask you to repeat them a couple of times because I somehow couldn't keep them straight. You repeated them, like a benign schoolteacher drilling his charge in essentials.

We came to another small clearing in the woods in the middle of which was one old and withered tree standing conspicuously alone, as if nothing else would grow near it. I told you that I had always seen this unusual tree as Dionysian, because its dark and gnarled trunk suggested something out of maenadic Greece, and because its location was so mysterious. But you looked puzzled, examined it closer, and found that the trunk twisted around until, at the bottom, it formed a kind of incredible serpent's head, with eyes and a mouth. I had never noticed this before, and was amused and astonished at what you had found. We both felt an awe about the place. How curiously separate the tree was from everything else, with its startling but undeniable serpent shape.

"I wouldn't be surprised," you said, "if there were an apple on this tree somewhere."

We looked up, and incredibly, near the top, there was one apple, the only one on the whole tree.

"Do you know what this place is?" you asked. "This is the Garden of Eden!"

We sat there awhile, in the Garden of Eden, and then moved on again. We came upon some boulders that had accumulated where there once was a house in Colonial times, long since burned out. The boulders were clustered and deep, suggesting a kind of shaft entrance.

"You're going to say this is the Gateway to the Underworld," I said, somewhat disrespectfully, and yet not entirely sure myself that it wasn't. You simply looked at me, then started peering down between the crevices as if you honestly expected to see something down there. There was nothing and we walked on.

Some cows were pastured nearby and we had to walk between them to keep our direction. They were a rather unusual breed. Perhaps it was only the reddening of a late afternoon sun, yet they all seemed to sport bizarre colors. Some seemed a shade of purple, others pink. We walked carefully through their midst since on another occasion I had been chased by a bull in this same place.

Finally we came out on the road on the other side of the woods. Across the road was a cemetery, not used since Colonial days. I started up the steps, holding up the plank that blocked the way, but you had already decided to climb over the stone wall. When I told you to come on here, that there were steps, you shouted back, "There's only one way to enter a cemetery, and it ain't that way!"

We walked around reading inscriptions on the gravestones, when you suddenly discovered one that you didn't want me to miss. You had to brush off some of the words to make it out:

> In memory of Mr. John
> Fletcher Who Died
> With ye Small-pox on ye
> 4th of August 1767 in ye
> 22nd year of his Age
>
> *When you behold this*
> *monument*
> *Consider how your*
> *Time is Spent*

Gravestones were of course very important sources of information for a poet whose chief subject was the history of a New England town. You had done a lot of cemetery exploration in Gloucester. Once, you said, you came upon a fallen gravestone in a deserted swamp there and decided to take it home with you to give it to the Gloucester Historical Society. You started carrying it, sweating heavily under its weight.

"I have too much surface for my apparatus," you said. "I have the insides of a baby and the surface of a giant. That's why I was sweating so heavily."

On the way home with the stone you started to pass the home of Carleton Coons, the anthropologist, who was a friend of yours.

"I was dying of thirst so I decided to stop at Coons' house for a drink. I went up and sat on his doorstep to rest. Old Coons came out and we started talking about the stone, but he didn't offer me a drink. And I didn't feel like asking. So after twenty minutes I picked up my stone again and went away. When I got to the road I suddenly realized that, Christ, I could be caught by the police and charged with stealing gravestones. So I left it hidden by the side of the road and drove my car back for it that night."

We decided to sit down on the stone wall at the back of the cemetery and rest. From nowhere, a cat suddenly ran along the wall until it reached you. It crawled around your shoulders, then started to play in and out with your legs. You responded as if it were an old friend. The cat paid no attention to me, though I was sitting next to you. I asked you where it came from, since I hadn't seen it before, and since it was a good distance from anyone's house.

"Where do you *think* it came from?" you said simply, implying that you were in on some mystery. We left it at that.

Farther up the road was a very old farmhouse, owned by an elderly farmer who lived there alone. Several windows of the house were broken, and the whole farm was in a state of disrepair, which added to its authenticity. In many ways it seemed the perfect New England farmhouse.

The farmer, Mr. Vargas, was crossing the road in front of his house, carrying two pails loaded with eggs. I had warned you, on the basis of previous encounters, that this man never said anything to anybody, except to make some wry crack about the weather in typical Yankee fashion. If I said that it was a cold day, he would always reply, "It'll get warmer." If I said it was warm, he would reply, "It'll get colder."

You stopped him with a hearty Olson hello and tried starting a conversation, admiring at first the cleanliness and plumpness of his roosters. The man just eyed you, but nodded to me. Then you asked him if his cows were not a special breed because of the incredibly strange colors they displayed.

"Just cows," the man clipped back.

You asked if one of the cows were sick, because it looked so spindly and weak and thin.

"That one's a calf," the man said.

I thought that would have been enough to stop you, but you dipped freely into one of his buckets and started examining his eggs. You tried to talk farm business and animal lore with him for the next ten minutes, asking complicated questions that he answered affably but with only a word. You finally released the man, whose arms must have been aching. As we walked away, you turned to me and lifted your eyebrows, as if you had just made a conversational conquest.

You kept remarking on the cleanliness of the place, as if you were an old hand at chicken farming.

"Chicken farming is dirty work," you said. "It's a filthy business, make no mistake about it."

You mentioned your own efforts at running a farm when Black Mountain College was in operation, and how difficult such problems were for you. You told me how the college had gone bankrupt under your rectorate, and how you had to sell the grounds to pay off all the creditors. The grounds consisted of 600 acres of "the most beautiful land in the Blue Ridge," as well as a herd of cattle, chickens, and pigs. Farming was really not one of your strong points.

I remembered a photograph of you pitching hay at Black Mountain, which you did on one occasion as a gesture to encourage the students to do farm work. The picture always reminded me of the annual photographs of Chairman Mao swimming in the Yangtze.

We walked on and came to a field filled only with an assortment of stones and rocks—an acre of them that had cropped up in such profusion that farming the land was impossible.

"For Christ's sake, Stonehenge too?" you asked, but my capacity for mythological fantasy was wearing thin by then, and we kept going.

We walked lazily back up the steep road to my house, with you picking up acorns from the side of the road, and stopping periodically to make some point or other. You kept telling me that this was paradise, and that I was an angel sent to guide you through it. I laughed at first, and felt flattered, but you kept repeating this. You would turn to me, hold your face about an inch from mine, which made me nervous, and demand to know if I was not in fact an angel sent to guide you through paradise. You insisted that I tell you the truth!

I knew that you had been studying the angelology of Ibn 'Arabi, the thirteenth-century Arab theologian and mystic, but I hardly expected you to apply it so locally. I told you that, as far as I knew, I wasn't an angel sent to guide you through this earthly paradise, or at least I didn't think I was.

"Are you absolutely sure?" you asked, with a wholly serious face that stunned me.

It was about five-thirty when we got back to the house. The walk had lasted three and a half hours. By the end of it, you had me half-disoriented by the mythological creation it had so easily become. We went inside and drank tea while you continued to exclaim on the wonders of paradise and I continued to be happily crazed by it all—by the imaginative dominion of this curious caliph that was Charles Olson.

Then you took a stone out of your pocket. You had picked it up in the woods somehow without my noticing. It was black with some white speckles on top. You gave it to me and said, "I want you to have this. This is the nicest thing I have to give you."

That night, on the back of a letter that I had written to you months before, and that for some reason you had brought with you to Connecticut, you wrote:

> In the order of time,
> each thing by itself (walking
> 3½ hours through the demesne
> of Miss Knowlton's hill and lake and other property,
> Wormwood Hill, (eastward on and from the
> Nipmuck Ranges north and south
> eastern and northern Connecticut fall
>   'LXIX (month September
>   specifically Saturday
>   September 27th

In only one day the land was yours.

How hard it is to remember those interminable conversations with you in my house. It was one continuous conversation, lasting for weeks, interrupted, reluctantly at first, only to sleep or when I had to leave for my classes. You were always ready to talk. There was no sane man who could match Olson as a talker. Your conversation was overwhelming.

It would be a two-way exchange, fast and easy, for the first few hours. Then, as my energy started to droop, you would actually pick up the pace, getting more and more intense as you saw me flagging. After several hours of listening to you talk in an increasingly booming voice about everything from poetry to cigars, I was exhausted.

It was too much for me. Sometimes you would talk for nine or ten hours straight. At first it was marvelous. I felt privileged to have the Olson genius all to myself at my table. But as the hours went on, and the days too, I couldn't keep up.

Furthermore, when friends would come to see me, you would go to the door and chase them away, though some of them didn't even know who you were. "Boer's busy and won't be able to see you for a few weeks," you'd shout at them.

When the telephone rang, interrupting a conversation, you would run to it and say, "He can't talk to you right now. Call back some other day." You would hang up before the other party could even say hello.

I didn't mind at first and god knows it was exciting! It was such a rare pleasure to have you, and I didn't think, then, that you would stay forever—although you scared me once when you asked if you could buy the house, hire a butler and maid, and both of us live here with your paying all the bills, "freeing you from all debts and expenses." I told you I didn't have any "debts and expenses" and that it didn't seem like such a good idea.

Sometimes, after hours of listening to you, when I just couldn't pay attention anymore, I would try to leave the table where we always talked, but you would grab my arm and keep me there or follow me wherever I managed to go in the house. I had to sit and listen. It began to seem like a great dizzying dream of words—all of them yours.

Sometimes you would write poems and notes in the early afternoon before getting out of bed. One day you wrote:

There's
too much knowledge. Thus
        of nothing, for
there is only possibly
one thing at a time only (the immrama)
one after another as such

        And each
takes a different
time or at least
a time of its own
        (order.
            O
        Thurs. Aft. 1:45
                Oct. 2
                Knowlton
                Hill
                1969

You wrote this after reading my copy of Geoffrey Ashe's *Land to the West,* a book about the medieval voyages of St. Brendan, called "Immrams." You didn't show me this poem, or even mention that you were writing poems at the time. If you had, I suppose I would have considered this one a desperate comment on the rush of knowledge that was pouring out of you then, so much faster than I could take it.

One night, when I managed to get away long enough to take a bath, you waited for me outside the bathroom door. Every few minutes you would call in for me to hurry up. "You're sure taking enough time in there," you shouted. "You must have really loved it as a baby!"

I think this last remark may have been triggered by a discussion we had just had about "Big Babies." I had a theory that all great politicians and artists (and artist-politicians) were "Big Babies" who had been spoiled terribly by their parents. Unlike mere "Spoiled Brats," "Big Babies" grew up to be absolute charmers in their social lives, though their charm was a lifelong continuation of babyhood and disguised an enormous ravening ego that secretly consumed everything and everyone. "Big Babies" always got their way. They were irresistible. They were fun. They managed to cast everyone else in the role of onlooking parent.

Lyndon Johnson was a "Big Baby" who went about The White House showing reporters all the documents marked "Top Secret" that only he was privileged to read.

Winston Churchill was a "Big Baby" who insisted on smoking cigars in the bathtub.

Picasso was a "Big Baby," and so were Orson Welles, Louis Armstrong, and Norman Mailer.

Ezra Pound was the "Big Baby" of poetry, but so, I said, were you. You laughed, at the time, and seemed flattered.

I had to keep thinking of plausible excuses to interrupt the conversation. Once, looking for a breather, I asked you if we could pause long enough to watch the news on television. You were reluctant—you were always reluctant because you so thoroughly enjoyed being convinced—but you finally agreed and then turned your head away, facing the opposite direction of the television set, intending to sit out and resume talking when the news was over. But then Walter Conkrite started ticking off the day's events and you slowly turned around to watch. You grew more and more interested. You expressed astonishment at "how fast those guys cover the news" though at the end of each minute's item you turned your head away again thinking that was it—only to turn back suddenly for the next item. You couldn't resist. Everything interested you. You wanted to know if it was like this every night.

Then President Nixon came on, and you were utterly fascinated.

"Is *that* Nixon?" you asked as if you had never seen him before.

You said you knew what he looked like but had never heard him speak.

The news of Washington reminded you of your own days there, and you recognized with amusement various faces from your own past, old Congressmen and bureaucrats.

Charles Olson starts his political adventures in 1941, working as publicity director for the American Civil Liberties Union in New York. In November of that year he moves to Chief of the Foreign Language Information Service for the Common Council for American Unity. A year later he begins working for the Office of War Information in Washington, and becomes associate chief of the Foreign Language Division. He has to write propaganda pamphlets on how well various nationality groups are serving the United States during the war. In one of these, called *Spanish-Speaking Americans in the War,* he collaborates with Ben Shahn, who paints a watercolor portrait of him. He works for the OWI until May of 1944, when he is hired as director of the Foreign Nationalities Division of the Democratic National Committee. Such jobs permit him to move in important government circles. He is becoming "established." President Roosevelt likes him.

Then, in 1945, he goes to Key West, Florida, for a brief vacation. He tells the following story later to his friends as the reason why he left government.

He is sitting in a room playing poker in Key West with several other men, all of them high Democratic Party functionaries, when the telephone rings. One man leaves to answer it and comes back exuberant, yelling, "We're in, boys, we're in!"

The man has just received news on the telephone of the death of President Roosevelt, and everyone is excited over the fact that Truman will now appoint all those present to top government posts. All the men at the table start rejoicing and discussing which posts they will acquire as loyal Trumanites.

Only Olson is silent. He sits there shocked. Gradually, the other poker players begin to notice that Charlie hasn't said anything. They try to cheer him up by telling him what posts he can expect. He will be offered the post of assistant secretary of the treasury. He will be offered the postmaster generalship! It is a tempting offer too, as they all know. Olson's father had been a postman who was driven to an early death in Worcester by the corrupt local postal hierarchy for his early attempts at unionizing the clerks. Olson considers taking the postmaster generalship if only to have the pleasure of firing the Worcester bosses. But he refuses all offers. The shock of this sudden demonstration of political greed is too much for him. He decides to quit the political world altogether and start writing again. He begins a final version of *Call Me Ishmael,* a book he finishes on August 6, 1945, the day Truman bombs Hiroshima.

But there is one more sally into the political arena, in 1948. Olson attends the Democratic National Convention as a supporter of Florida's Senator Claude Pepper for president. Pepper loses his bid for the presidency, and in 1950 loses his bid for reelection to the Senate when his opponent, George Smathers, calls him "the Red Pepper" in a celebrated early case of Cold War vitriol. Ironically, Richard Nixon models his own campaign for the Senate in 1950 on that of his good friend, Smathers, using the same approach that Smathers has used on "the Red Pepper" to defeat his own opponent, Congresswoman Helen Gahagan Douglas, whom Nixon calls "the Pink Lady." The American political scene is beginning a decade of exquisite viciousness. It is no place for a poet, and Olson gets out once and for all.

About a month after this introduction to television news at my house, you told me that when you returned to Gloucester you bought a television set yourself, adding that yours was much better than mine because yours was color.

Dishes, meanwhile, were piled high in the sink. There was never any time to clean up with you there. There was never time to do anything.

One Sunday afternoon, when there wasn't a clean spoon to be had in the house, I formally asked your permission to do the dishes, leaving you alone for awhile to sit looking out the window onto the hillside. To entertain you during this lapse, since we had been talking about music and especially the music of Stravinsky, I put a Stravinsky record on for you, followed by a recording by Pierre Boulez, with whom you had once corresponded. The recording was Boulez' *Le Marteau sans Maître*.

You listened patiently and seemed to enjoy the record very much, often exclaiming your pleasure at the unusual tones of the soprano. ("Wow!") But when it finished, you walked into the kitchen and announced that there was something wrong with it. You thought awhile, and then said it was because Boulez was "divided against himself." You went back and made a note to this effect on the record sleeve, adding at the bottom:

> (Knowlton Hill's (dining-room's) like)
> living on the earth as though it were a planet!
> for Chas, for it, Chas

After the Boulez record, I asked you if you wouldn't mind listening something of a different sort, and got out a Bob Dylan record. It was *Nashville Skyline* and you took to it immediately. You started laughing at the lyrics and then dancing. When it finished, you made me play it over again, and then again. You broke up laughing each time a song came on.

You were particularly amused by "Lay, Lady, Lay." You would reply to the words, make jokes about "country pie" and continue dancing to it.

Your favorite on the album was the song about "Peggy Day" and "Peggy Night," which you asked me to play at least a half-dozen times. Though the volume was turned up, you leaned down to the floor, where the speakers were, to make sure that you were getting every word. You memorized the song, and called Dylan "a master."

When you asked me who the piano player was, and I told you that that too was Dylan, you refused to believe it. You refused to believe that Dylan was *that* good, and though I assured you he was, you went to the telephone and called a friend in Massachusetts to ask him if he knew if Bob Dylan played the piano part on the *Nashville Skyline* album. He told you it was true, and you were even more delighted. I asked you if you wanted to hear some earlier Dylan albums, and you said, "Yeah, this is too good to be true!"

I brought out the *John Wesley Hardin* album and put that on. You listened but were not at all impressed. "He just didn't have it then," you said.

It was so hard for you to go to bed before four or five in the morning, just as it was hard for you to get up before two or three in the afternoon (and sometime six). And you were brilliantly resourceful in stalling me from going to bed at one or two a.m., though by then I was often asleep in my chair.

You hated to have people read (or even show) their poetry to you. One night, however, after I had said goodnight and started for my room, you suddenly asked me what I was writing. I told you about my long narrative poem, *Varmint Q*, about William Clarke Quantrill and his Civil War escapades. You asked me to read you some of it.

I ran to get it out, excited at the opportunity of having you hear it. I no sooner began to read you the first chapter, however, when you started laughing boisterously. While it was supposed to be funny, you seemed to be overdoing it. I said I was going to bed if you didn't stop.

"Don't be so touchy," you said.

You offered corrections for some lines, and told me to take some out. You said I should call the style of the poem "the annalic."

"The story is the poem," you said. "The narrative is the poem. Keep to the narrative and don't wander off."

One of the lines had Quantrill asking a card dealer to take a card by saying, "Take a nap, pard."

You asked me what a "nap" was, and when I explained, you said, "That word is yours from now on."

You pleased me very much when you said that you liked it. Then you said suddenly that *you* were going to finish it for me.

"How could you do that?" I asked. "You don't have my sources."

"That don't matter," you replied.

I explained that I planned to work on it for at least another year, that it was to be an epic, and that I thought you of all people would understand, since your own *Maximus Poems* went on and on as a long-range project.

"Don't be so presumptuous," you replied.

At one point you interrupted me to ask if the letters of Quantrill that I was quoting in the poem were exact quotations, or if I had "touched them up."

I said that I had touched them up only slightly.

"I understand," you said. "I do the same thing."

I read to you for about an hour, and then we talked about poetry for awhile. It must have been three or four o'clock in the morning. When it seemed that you had nothing more to say on the subject, I said good night and started for my room again.

"Well, fuck you," you said abruptly. "Read a poem like that and then just go to bed. What do you think this is?"

I stayed a little longer, until you grudgingly gave it up for that night.

One night during your first week in Mansfield we were invited to dinner at the home of Charles and Kay Brover. Brover had been one of your students at Buffalo and was now teaching English at the University of Connecticut. He was also serving as faculty advisor to the local SDS chapter. In the turbulent fall of 1968 and the following spring, Brover participated in a number of political demonstrations at the university. These demonstrations were against on-campus recruiting by the Dow Chemical Company, and against the R.O.T.C., as well as other Vietnam-related organizations. A climax, of sorts, came in an hour-long program on national television, in which Brover presented the case for the radicals, and the president of the university defended the administration.

You had not seen Brover in several years and you were anxious to know "what he had done with himself as a result of my instruction!"

It was a happy reunion, "just like the old days," you kept saying, remembering the nights you used to spend with the Brovers on Custer Street in Buffalo, when we were putting together a magazine called *The Niagara Frontier Review.* The magazine was originally intended to utilize the sudden "hotness" of the Niagara region. You were to be a contributing editor from Buffalo, and had planned to get as editors Marshall McLuhan from Toronto, who had not yet published *Understanding Media,* and Norman O. Brown from Rochester. McLuhan, however, had rejected the idea, saying he was beyond any interest in avant-garde little magazines anymore, and Brown, for some reason, never got involved either.

At dinner that night you were extremely excited, talking powerfully, and at one point you slammed your fist down on the Brovers' glass tabletop and smashed it to pieces. You quickly said you were sorry, offered to pay for it, then went right on talking, putting the tablecloth back so that it hid the big pieces of glass that now rested on everyone's laps.

After dinner, in the living room, you argued amiably with Brover on the merits of his political position. It was nonetheless a spirited debate on both sides. Brover recited a list of the board of trustees at the University of Connecticut and the numerous interlocking corporations and banks they also represented. You argued back that you knew "all that stuff" and "who are you kidding?" This was not the place for attack, you insisted.

"What is the place for attack then?" Brover asked, but you never gave him a direct reply.

Several students had drifted in by now and were sitting on the floor listening. In the students' eyes, you seemed to have won the debate, if only because of an unremitting aura of self-confidence you gave off. Yet your own politics as they involved these issues didn't really come out, and you weren't very clear at all as to what your own course was.

You demanded to know, rather blusterously at one point, why you had not received copies of the local SDS publication, *The UCONN Free Press*. "Don't you know I receive *all* underground newspapers? Why haven't I received yours?"

My impression was that you felt a kinship with contemporary radical politics only so far as it resembled your own life-style of the past twenty years. You thoroughly admired radical youth and seemed to identify with them, although you rarely, if ever, did anything publicly with political issues. You never signed your name to anything of a political nature, except on one occasion, which involved the arrest of your friend, LeRoi Jones. I assumed this was because you thought your own writing was radicalism enough. As a "radical poet," you could forego any other public kind of commitment.

You weren't very particular in your criticism of the multiple kinds of radical action that were then developing. It was one life-style, and I'm sure you thought it was your own. But your own politics were vague, even when one tried to pin you down. You seemed beyond taking the subject seriously. It was as if your political activities of the Thirties and Forties had cured you forever of the bug.

I can remember a time in the early Sixties when we thought for awhile that you might even have been a Republican because of your contempt for President Kennedy. Political innocents, we were all Kennedy enthusiasts then, and only Republicans, it seemed, bitter losers, denounced the man. It never occurred to us then that there was a third alternative.

Once, when I pried it out of you that Kennedy had been a student of yours at Harvard when you were a tutor there in American Studies, I asked you excitedly what he was like.

"Oh, he was a C student, just a C student," you said nonchalantly.

"Well did you at least keep his papers?" I asked for some absurd reason.

"I never keep a C paper," you replied.

After dinner at the Brovers, you kept grumbling all the way home about Brover's politics. You said the SDS girls, who "just hang around for the action," were "cheap Commie fucks, that's all they are, we used to have a lot of them in the Thirties, nothing but cheap Commie fucks!"

At the same time, though, Brover told me that you called him afterward, to thank him for the dinner, and also to tell him, "There's just the three of us, Brover, just the three of us: you, me, and John Wieners."

And shortly after this, you told one of your graduate students, Mark Zaitchik, about your night at the Brover house. "I walked into Brover's," you said, "and he started giving me the party line, so I said to him, 'Where's *your work,* boy,' and slammed down my fist and broke his fucking table!"

Your only voiced criticism of radicalism was that American radicals were not really out to win. You were afraid that they would settle for something less than victory—and you were always on the side of the winners in history.

When I visited you in Gloucester in May of 1969, some thirty students at Dartmouth had just been arrested and were serving terms in jail. You were extremely pleased with them.

"Kids today are beating America by moving aside from it," you said. But then you found in a newspaper account that the students had been "allowed" their books to study with in jail, and they had accepted the offer. This later development incensed you. You didn't want them to give in to the conventional expectations of good students in jail. On the other hand, when I suggested that many of the kids you praised so generally had "moved aside" only to find increased frustration in their lives, you suddenly agreed.

"Yeah," you said, "they think they'll live forever. They think you can actually do something good for this country if you work at it long enough. They don't have enough ego. You've got to have a lot of ego."

There were two events of 1969 that you came back to again and again that night at Brover's: the gathering of young people at Woodstock and the astronauts' trip to the moon. You thought of these events as of the utmost significance.

I was surprised at first at your interest in the moon-shot, though in retrospect I shouldn't have been. I was an enthusiast myself, in spite of all the people I knew who thought it was an arrogant waste of money.

You talked about it almost with a child's awe. While I was impressed with Armstrong and his staggering simplicity as a hero, you were more impressed with Aldrin, who was the coupler of the two ships. You said that Aldrin had written a dissertation at MIT on coupling, and that he was the world expert on the subject, which was why he was chosen for the job. You were very interested in the implications of this—that the man who was the world's theoretical expert should at the same time become the man who actually made the physical coupling in space. It meant something to you in terms of the possibilities of "total knowledge."

Most of your information on the space program came from Norman Mailer's articles in *Life*, which you said were not only the finest things Mailer ever wrote, but the prose itself was of a new order—talking of devils and gods and with a cosmological awe worthy of Charles Olson himself!

For years you were a devoted reader of *Scientific American*; you followed developments in the space program, kept up with news of the astronauts, and read scientific reports with considerable interest. On the other hand, earlier in the year in Gloucester, you told me that you had been invited by a man who was planning to edit an anthology of poems about "outer space" to submit some of your own "space" poems.

"Imagine the stupidity," you said, "thinking the astronauts were into something that we, as poets, don't already know." And you said that you wrote to the editor telling him to publish your poem, "Dogtown IV," if he wanted to know about the subject, but that "it was a stupid idea."

When I jokingly suggested that they publish your letter rather than your poem, you said, "Of course, but they're not that smart, those guys."

On another occasion, you told us how you had once invited Jung to lecture at Black Mountain College during the Fifties. Jung had declined the invitation because of bad health and had sent instead a young lady from the Jung Institute in Zurich, Marie-

Louise Von Franz, who lectured on aphids and how they die with the plant they live on. You commented that man's moving to the moon suddenly was like the aphid moving to another plant. And you slurred deliberately on the words "plant" and "planet."

Woodstock intrigued you as well. The Brovers had themselves gone to it, only to be dismayed and discouraged by the miles of traffic jams. Brover, stinging perhaps from your earlier attack on his politics, and not sharing at all your view of pan-hippieism as the key to our national salvation, goaded you by saying, "Yeah, Charles, I'm surprised you didn't go to it yourself—all your people were there."

You replied calmly, if mysteriously, that you were out at sea that day, in a boat off Gloucester, and you heard voices from the direction of Woodstock calling to you, summoning you like Sirens to the festival. But you couldn't go.

I mentioned to my chairman in the English Department, William Moynihan, that you were visiting me, and he asked me if you were interested in a job at the university. I told him that I didn't think so because of the many offers you had received since leaving Buffalo, none of which you ever accepted, and besides, you were still in effect only on leave from the Buffalo faculty—even if it had been four years.

That night at dinner I casually brought the matter up. "My chairman wanted to know today if you would be interested in a job here," I said.

"And what did you tell him?" you shot back.

"I said that I didn't think you would, because you had a number of offers and never accepted them."

"Well, you go right back and tell your chairman that I *am* interested," you said.

What a surprise that was. For nearly five years you had been living a life of productive solitude in Gloucester. I thought you would never want to go back to teaching again. Now, for some reason, you did.

The offer of a job, however, was meant for the following semester (we were already a few weeks into the fall semester). But you said you would accept an appointment only if it would be made to begin immediately. Otherwise, you said, you were thinking of taking off for Crete for the winter. And you wanted to know if I would be willing to take a leave of absence—in the middle of the semester—to accompany you on this venture, which you called "an archaeological expedition."

I took you to meet Moynihan at his house. Bill and Ruth introduced you to their numerous children, and you talked to each one with great attention. One of their sons, who was running for high school class president, was rehearsing a campaign speech. You demanded to hear the speech. As a former high school debater, whose speaking prowess had won a national prize (a trip to Europe) that was awarded by Herbert Hoover (who sat in for President Coolidge), you were ready to offer expert advice on the art of public speaking.

Afterwards, Moynihan told me how much he liked you, "if for no other reason than Olson's the only person other than myself who ever remembered all my kids' names."

He asked you where you would live while teaching here. There was a sudden pause, so I said, in jest, that I would move out of my house and you could live there.

Later that night, you said, "By the way, that was very kind of you to offer to move out of our house for me."

I had to explain that I had only been kidding.

At first it looked impossible that funds could be found on such short notice for your salary.

"They should hire me immediately and find the money later," you said.

You decided then that it was all over and you were preparing to leave. You had even written a farewell note to me, which you left on my desk. I found the note and thought you had left, but you had merely gone to sleep in your room. The note said:

> Charlie—
> It was all
> *treat* and it was worth a million bucks. O.

Along with the note was a check for twenty-five dollars for long-distance telephone calls.

I pleaded with you to give us more time to find the money. In the meantime, Moynihan asked you for a *curriculum vitae,* a bureaucratic necessity for deans and provosts. While I was out one evening, you phoned George Butterick in Pennsylvania and asked George to prepare one for you. George had been a student of yours at Buffalo, where he wrote his dissertation on *The Maximus Poems.*

When you told George that you would be working for the University of Connecticut, and to send the *curriculum vitae* to the chairman there, whom you referred to as "a good and fair Irishman," George too was surprised. He asked you why you chose Connecticut. Why not Buffalo again?

You replied jokingly that Charlie Brover and the SDS had cleared the way for you at Connecticut by almost causing the president to resign. "Maybe I could even be president," you said.

"What would you want to be that for?" George joked. "Why a university president? Why not president of the United States? You know you had a chance a year and a half ago when that coalition of hippie groups approached you to run."

"Do you really believe that?" you asked.

"Sure!" George said, not expecting you to get serious all of a sudden.

"I just as well might, the poor job of it Nixon is doing," you said.

The two of you talked for a long time. You told him how agreeable the Connecticut air was for you. You asked George if he would be interested in staying at your apartment in Gloucester, since you wouldn't be using it and George might want to work there. After a while George began to get worried about the cost of the phone call, and he asked where you were calling from.

"I'm at Charlie Boer's, and he won't mind," you said. "He's gone out with some friends for the evening."

At about that point I came home. I had merely gone across the street for a few minutes. I tried to open the living room door but you had locked it. You quickly told George that you had to hang up because you could hear me coming, and that you would call him later. George thought you sounded worried that I would find you on the phone and for some reason be angry. When you finally let me into the living room, you said nothing about the phone call and pretended that you had locked the door accidentally. A strange business, Mr. Olson.

At the end of the week, several of us made an urgent visit to the provost's office to argue your case. We wanted you to come too, but you declined, preferring to spend that morning in bed. I armed myself with my entire collection of your books, and a photograph, and placed them all in a scattered pile on the provost's desk. He was impressed, but explained what we already knew—it was hard to find funds in the middle of the semester.

I told him what a once-in-a-lifetime opportunity this was for the University of Connecticut. Moynihan told him that you felt you should be hired immediately and the funds found later.

There was a pause. "He's absolutely right, of course," the provost said suddenly, and you were hired. You would start the following week.

When I told you all this later you said, "Hell, I don't want to be a professor, I want to be a fucking provost!"

The course you were to teach was for graduate students only. You gave it several titles at first, and had drawn up an elaborate description to show to Moynihan, who came out to my house along with a colleague, Jack Davis, to talk to you about it. The first title that you proposed to them had to do with "the origins of the Thames and Connecticut rivers." Moynihan listened with a straight face. Ultimately you proposed a course in early English and the influence of Norse mythology, a subject that you were working on for several years, to judge by the copious notes on Norse myth in some of your journals.

I wasn't home when they came out to the house to meet you that afternoon, but when I did return I found the kitchen cleaned up, the dishes done, and everything neatly put away. I told you you didn't have to do all that, but you were in a glowing mood and said, "It was a pleasure. And anyway, everything should be in order when the boss comes to visit."

You were no bug for order though, in any conventional sense. Your own apartment in Gloucester always had piles of books and papers scattered around everywhere. But it was usually clean and well-swept, which you took care of yourself. And once, when a friend good-naturedly straightened up the books and papers for you when you were away on a trip, you were vehement. There was an order to it all that only you knew.

Many people seemed to welcome the impression, based on your easygoing manner, that you must have been careless about your living conditions as well. They saw you as some kind of super-Bohemian poet with a truck driver's vocabulary and tastes. Nothing could be further from the truth. You referred to this as "the Victor McLaglen syndrome," where big guys like yourself automatically get typed as bulls in china shops. In fact, you were always an astonishingly gentle man, managed very well in china shops, and the deep-voiced Wallace Beery boom of your "fuck this" and "fuck that" sat so comfortably on you (*nobody* could swear so masterfully as Charles Olson!) that one didn't really notice it after the first few astounding moments.

It was all very natural, because you were so natural. You ac-

44

quired your gift for obscenities, you once said, from all the talking you used to do with Gloucester fishermen.

"We have to use obscenities in this country," you said, "to be fine at all, or to be mandarin at least." And fine and mandarin you were.

After you read your course proposal to Moynihan and Davis that afternoon, you discussed salary with them. You knew that Stephen Spender was presently teaching at the university as Writer-in-Residence, and so you announced that you didn't want that title. You would be Visiting Professor. And though there had already been great difficulty in getting any funds at all to pay you on such short notice, you now announced that you wouldn't take the job "for anything less than what Stephen Spender is getting. He's not worth half as much as I am!"

You wanted to settle here, you told them, because "this is the changing time in my life." You had been so bothered by illnesses and problems, you said, that you decided a change was all you needed. It was "a return, a fulfillment" for you. You told them that you had been working on the material for the course for the past eight years, and you were now ready to spring it all.

You were keenly interested in the number of students you would have in this course. Moynihan explained that in seminars for graduate students it was customary to limit enrollment to twelve, but in graduate lectures the enrollment was open to twenty.

"I like twelve," you said.

I remember very well taking you to your first class. You crammed several large wicker baskets with paper and books, two of which I carried behind you as you walked down the hall to the classroom. Things kept falling out of the baskets, and we stopped a couple of times to pick them up, or, rather, I stopped, because while you moved slowly, you were like a great ship whose momentum couldn't be altered. You would simply smile as things fell out of the baskets, knowing they would be picked up.

When we finally got to the door of the classroom, you went in, I behind you. You looked at the class. They stared back with the usual astonishment at your size. I then turned to leave, quietly wishing you luck, and walked out the door. But you turned too, right behind me, and followed me out into the hall. I laughed and told you to go back in, that this was *it*. Nervously, you told me to be sure and come back for you at 6:30. I assured you I would, and you finally went in.

I returned promptly at 6:30, two and a half hours later. When I went in to get you, you said, "What do *you* want?"

"It's 6:30," I said.

"Come back in an hour," you said, and went right on with what looked like a great time.

As soon as I left, you turned to the class and said, "That Boer!"

In spite of your nervousness, or maybe because of it, you came on very tough that first day, Professor Olson. You walked over to the table in the center of the room, looked scornfully at it, quickly ran your finger over it to check for dust, then screamed, "Somebody clean off this fucking table!"

The students were scared to death. A girl bravely got up and dusted it off for you.

Then you tried to scare away anyone who was there only as a tourist. And you were successful, perhaps too successful. You said you wanted no poet types in the class, only scholars. And absolutely no one but bona fide graduate students. One student was even reprimanded for knowing only Attic Greek and not Homeric Greek, and dismissed.

Then you got rid of some of the women in the class with a long blast of the foulest language you could muster. This was a tactic you had used effectively at Buffalo, I recall. You hated the middle-aged schoolteachers who took your class only for the three credits it would give them and didn't suspect for a minute when they signed up what a withering assault on their innocence the class would be. Your initial blasts were fair warning. Unfortunately, it all backfired on you this time. The most interesting faces in the room (the undergraduates) and the prettiest, you said, got up and left.

When you saw what a dreadful lot you were left with, you sent a student out into the hall to ask one particularly attractive girl to come back.

"Where did she go?" you asked. "I didn't mean her." Unfortunately, she refused to come back or to have anything further to do with you.

You asked each student his name, where he was from, and why he wanted to take the course. You told them to plan on committing themselves to work with you for at least the next two years. At the end of that time, they were to have something published as a result of the course.

The students were amused as you dipped periodically into one of your wicker baskets during the class to eat a Keebler cookie, washing it down with cup after cup of machine-dispensed black coffee or equally thin machine-dispensed chicken soup. You had notes and scrawls written on your shirtsleeves, on your cuffs, on matchbooks, and in books divided with toilet paper bookmarks. Sometimes, in a frenzy, you gobbled up your tie like Oliver Hardy in crisis. When students asked you to open the windows, you refused, saying you hated fresh air.

You were particularly hard on students who opposed your views in class. You didn't believe at all in the classroom as a place for the free exchange of ideas. Your classroom was for your ideas. If a student thought otherwise, he was soon set straight on the matter. Sometimes you would argue a point strenuously and at length only to have a student refute it with a simple fact you didn't know. When this happened, you dropped the subject immediately as if it weren't worth continuing, and went on with something else.

One day you were discussing phenomenology and Husserl's views on the nature of time. Mark Zaitchik raised his hand like a good student and tried to present the case for logical positivism.

"Well, there's one in every class," you said abruptly, and dismissed the subject entirely. Instead, you started talking about literary symbolism. At one point you couldn't remember the author of a key book on the subject.

"Who wrote that fucking book on symbolism in American literature?" you asked. Zaitchik again raised his hand and said that it was Charles Feidelson. "You would know," you said grudgingly, and then dropped that subject too.

You appointed another student, Oliver Ford, "the class bibliographer." He was to write down the titles of all the books you mentioned in class.

One day, as he was busily writing, you came up behind him, grabbed his shoulders, and pressed down so hard that he couldn't move. "You got that?" you asked.

You told them that Yeats, a poet you didn't like, was nonetheless such a great figure that "you have to hoof him in the ass or you'll never be nothing."

You said the same of Picasso. "Hoof him in the ass too."

Someone then suggested that you were a great figure too, and that they were all being influenced by you. What about you?

"Of course," you said. "Hoof me in the ass too."

Throughout the course, you recited passages of Shakespeare from memory, especially from *King Lear*. One day you recited "Sonnet 76," which was apparently your favorite:

> Why is my verse so barren of new pride,
> So far from variation or quick change?
> Why with the time do I not glance aside
> To new-found methods and to compounds strange?
> Why write I still all one, ever the same,
> And keep invention in a noted weed,
> That every word doth almost tell my name,
> Showing their birth and where they did proceed?
> O, know, sweet love, I always write of you,
> And you and love are still my argument;
> So all my best is dressing old words new,
> Spending again what is already spent:
> > For as the sun is daily new and old,
> > So is my love still telling what is told.

The students soon realized that this was to be the freest class they had ever taken. One of them decided to bring a couple of bottles of wine to class, to loosen things up even more. One was a bottle of Almaden Chablis, the other a New York State wine. You were offered first choice and took the Almaden, saying it was the best white wine produced in America, while the New York State was the worst. During the class, you kept the Almaden all to yourself, while the students got the New York State whether they liked it or not.

You drank the whole bottle, and your lecture that day seemed the least coherent of all. The student who brought it resolved never to bring wine again.

You chain-smoked cigarettes or your pipe throughout the class. There were frequent emphysematous bursts of coughing and hacking.

Once as you reached across the table for one of Mark Zaitchik's Marlboros, he grabbed your hand with a well-intentioned gesture and said, "You've had enough."

You simply glared at him, then took the whole pack and smoked them all.

As the room became dense with smoke, one student ran to the window and opened it saying, "I don't care, I've got to have something to breathe."

Wrapped up in my old army blanket, you reiterated your policy against fresh air. But she insisted that she was suffocating.

"Okay, but for just a little while," you said. You stood at the window and closed it again within the minute.

One student was from Norway, and this was her first class in an American university. You treated her as an expert on Norse mythology and language and turned to her occasionally for support by asking, "Ain't that right, Eva? Ain't that right, Eva baby?"

She said later that she didn't understand anything you were talking about and that she didn't like your course at all.

Behind all the eccentricities, however, most students found a more than substantial teacher. One of them, John Cech, was so impressed after the first class that he wrote to a friend telling him "how completely overpowering Olson was, unlike anything in common academe. But with the most startling patience and kindness tempting you from ignorance. This all sounds devotional. But what meat!"

Another student said that he was so totally bored with graduate school that he was planning to drop out until he took your course. You redeemed everything.

The emphasis of the course was on Icelandic and Skaldic narrative poetry, rather than English. Our language, our condition, you found more traceable to "the North Atlantic currents" than to England. In the Norse sagas, you told them, Indo-European cosmology surfaced once more, two thousand years after Hesiod. And at the same time that Norse bards were practicing their craft in the cold Northlands, the Arabs were opening an important second front on the same subject in the desert. You told the class that "the immediate condition" of their language was in Frisian, in runes, and eddas, in Egil and Snorri. And you kept emphasizing the students' own location at that moment, "up the road from Four Corners" in Mansfield. You compared them to "the pre-English tributaries of the Thames" in Connecticut. The subject of the course was poetics, but to get at poetics, you told them, they had to learn about language. They had to "imagine words inside." You wanted them to see themselves as "the agents of stories," as "mythologists," which was how you saw yourself. Our condition now, you argued, is one of illiteracy, where what matters is not whether you can read, as whether you can write. You told them to be "scribes"—to concentrate on "the applicableness of what you know." For this reason, you said, you were "an enemy of mantras, mandalas, and symmetry." You were a Tantrist, and for a Tantrist "life is a book." You believed in the Arab concept of "Ta wil"— that you walk leftwards "to meet the angel of your own being who is walking backwards until you pass through and become yourself." You recommended to them *The Meccan Revelations* of Ibn 'Arabi. By "Ta wil," you said, you "retard eternity." You fall back into the world. You called this act of falling, "precarity"—involving the loss of one's own identity. Again and again you would tell them to fall back into the world, and to fall back into the word. Mythology was not reference, not metaphor, it was "an inner inherence" that one had to learn in order to give oneself control over time and space, "the retardation of eternity." It was in this sense that you were a poet, you declared, because "poetry is the articulation of order."

Your apparent nervousness at resuming a teaching role reminded me of the day I met you. It was in a classroom at the State University of New York at Buffalo in 1963. Several years had elapsed since you left Black Mountain College, years spent mostly in Gloucester where, with your wife, Betty, and son, Charles Peter, you lived in poverty.

Albert Cook, who had just been named chairman of the English Department at Buffalo, called to offer you a job. You told me later how breathless you and your wife were as Cook talked to you about the terms of the appointment. You said that, with fingers crossed, you were planning to hold out for what you thought would be a good salary—a thousand dollars! When Cook offered more than fifteen times that amount, you nearly fell off your chair, you said, and then replied, as calmly as you could, "I accept."

I had transferred to the Graduate School in Comparative Literature at Buffalo from Harvard, and it was my first day too. The room for your seminar in "Myth and Poetics" was in the basement of Crosby Hall. Steam pipes lined the ceiling. Some old tables were piled high on top of each other in a dingy corner. A proto-hippie type, the first I had ever seen, sat down on the topmost table near the ceiling, lurking there, casting a cold eye down on the rest of us—an odd bunch ourselves. Some were from the old, more conservative, Buffalo English Department (before it became the State University). Some had followed you there from Canada after a conference in Vancouver that summer. And some were like myself, plunked down in this strange country for no particular reason. The university was soon to blossom into the most exciting and outrageous school in the United States in poetry, music, and the arts, but on that first day, waiting for the mysterious Charles Olson, it all seemed a little absurd, the last place in the world for the Muse to come.

You walked in that rainy afternoon wearing a full-length Gloucester fisherman's cape. You put a tape recorder down in the middle of the table and, without saying a word, played your poems for us. I was amazed at your size and manner—and surprised by your poems too, which I had not read before. You prowled around the table as we listened, all trying to look, I think, like serious students. I smiled at the strangeness of it all. You made several slow circles of the table and then stopped somewhere behind my back. I kept staring ahead, trying hard to concentrate on your poems, but almost laughing now at the somber kid sitting high above us all on the tables in the corner. Suddenly you opened your huge cape and half-enclosed me in it, your foot pulling on the back rung of my chair. With your cape hanging in front of me, I could barely see. This has got to be one of the nuttiest places I've ever been, I said to myself, and finally laughed out loud. Fortunately, you laughed too and it broke the nervousness of the situation. Later, you told me that you were so terrified that morning when you started out for class that your wife told you to just go in and play the tape recorder and if somebody smiled, make friends with him.

Your class soon became the most exciting event of the week for me. I never knew what to expect. Though you always appeared in a jacket and tie, your manner was as casual as a cab driver's. You would be so casual in fact that it was often difficult, for the first hour or so, to see what you were getting at in your lecture. You could be incredibly funny, as when you would do your lumbering imitations of the great bear dance, romping around the desk and whooping like an Indian. You could just as easily silence the lot of us with a burst of angry remarks about what poor excuses for graduate students we were if we couldn't recite for you a passage from *Two Noble Kinsmen*.

Once you went on for three baffling weeks talking at random about metaphor and Manhattan and gesture and time and the self. No one could figure out what you were driving at, though it was apparent you were becoming increasingly intense and that it was all leading to something. What it was leading up to, it turned out, was a magnificent reading of Whitman's poem "Crossing Brooklyn Ferry." Your voice dropped to a magisterial depth and richness. I had never heard anything like it. And as you brought alive the majesty of those passages you would pause every few seconds, lift your glasses above those fat, hairy brows, and look at each one of us for an assurance that we understood exactly what you, and Whitman, were saying:

> It avails not, time nor place—distance avails not,
> I am with you, you men and women of a generation,
>   or ever so many generations hence,
> Just as you feel when you look on the river and sky,
>   so I felt,
> Just as any of you is one of a living crowd,
>   I was one of a crowd,
> Just as you are refresh'd by the gladness of the river
>   and the bright flow, I was refresh'd,
> Just as you stand and lean on the rail, yet hurry with
>   the swift current, I stood yet was hurried,
> Just as you look on the numberless masts of ships
>   and the thick-stemm'd pipes of steamboats, I look'd.

It was as if you became Walt Whitman. This was his voice. If you had suddenly produced old Walt himself waiting in the wings I would not have been more impressed. Olson and Whitman were suddenly one. We were all suddenly one. Everything that you had been talking about for the past three weeks became clear and meaningful in that one moment. I doubt that any actor or any other poet and certainly no other teacher could have read that poem with such authority. Charles Olson, I realized that afternoon, was a master.

I once asked you, in a letter, what the secret was of your ability to read poetry aloud so splendidly. How did you do it? You replied, simply, that David Tudor, the pianist, had told you how to read. I then had to send another letter, as you knew I would, to ask you what David Tudor had said. You replied:

And as of Tudor all he sd to me [when I was in my usual difficulties reading what's written out loud—at least if it's my own]—all thus was the 1st reading, & from proofs, of 1-10, & a 2nd night (when I *tried* to apply the lesson—& not too successfully) of 11–22—Black Mountain, Summer 1953—what David as a very knowing pianist, & who had already I believe convinced me that same summer of what a pianist can do when he can read a score—indeed, what it took for him to find out how to read Boulez' script of the *Deuxieme Sonate* [it took Artaud's poems!] all David sd was read what's written on the page. Wow!

On the back of the envelope of this letter you added the following:

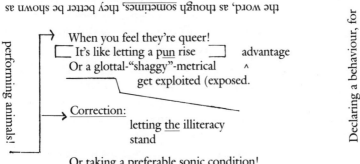

In spite of how impressed I was with your performance in class, I found your own poems extremely difficult when I first read them. They demanded a knowledge of matters I knew little, if anything, about—Mayan and Sumerian myths, odd moments in

American Colonial history, mathematics, Red Cloud, the history of Gloucester, Massachusetts. Your poems seemed to expect more of the reader than those of any poet I had ever read (if they *expected* anything at all). To read Olson, one had to read your sources, a task that seemed fathomless.

And the way you spaced the words out on the page—"Projective Verse"—was also a novelty for me. One day we managed to get you talking in class about "Projective Verse," a subject everyone was of course very interested in, but which you seemed rather tired of. You seemed to feel that the term had become too easy a tag for you, and that people were making too much of it. You called our attention to Mallarmé's Preface to *Un Coup de Dés,* where you said we would find much the same view as your own.

You talked of your work, and of yourself, as "post-modern," or "post-literary." Your purpose in writing was not the making of "literature." From the vantage point of the post-literary, the rules and directions of anything "literary" were obsolete. Such a position is beyond conventional criticism, which of course remains "literary." "No Greek will be able to discriminate my body," your poem goes. This was not arrogance, I think, so much as it was self-interest in the best sense. You saw poetry, the primary mode of expression in all pre-literary societies, as your own best post-literary means of knowing and articulating order. And though like many poets you seemed to read little actual contemporary poetry, in your case, I think, it was not from narrowness of vision. It was because so few contemporaries, busy being "artists," seemed to *know* anything worth saying to you.

The art of saying something well in verse just wasn't enough, in itself, to interest you. When you would, rarely, come upon some literary piece, a poem or book of poems sent to you (you *never* bought any), the adjective you almost invariably used to describe it (dismiss it) was "handsome." "A handsome piece of work." "Handsomely done." "A very handsome job." This word described what you thought most other people worked at their art for—a kind of cleverness, subtlety, or well-wrought craft. For others, poetry was the art of expressing oneself "handsomely." Your own work was of another order altogether. The proper response to it was some expression of surprise or disbelief or astonishment at the discovery of some "fact." "Beautiful" was never the right adjective for someone to use as a description of your work. There were certain words, common enough, that rarely entered your vocabulary. "Beautiful" was one of them. With you it was almost a term of contempt, connoting "a waste of time."

Olson, you were doomed from the start to be plagued by baffled readers like myself who didn't realize, or refused to accept, so novel a way of doing a thing called verse. But you never seemed to mind.

While taking courses with you at Buffalo, I was at the same time writing a doctoral dissertation on *The Bacchae* of Euripides. The subject didn't interest you at all, again because it was "literary" and I was writing it as conventional literary criticism. You kept urging me to give all that up and join you in Second Millennium studies. In your opinion, there was no value whatsoever in another academic look at Euripides. It was time to study the (unfortunately nonexistent) literature of prehistoric Crete.

You kept firing notes and postcards at me to this effect. The return address on one of these told it all:

Situation Crete 1500
Charles Olson
Wyoming, New York

Dear Charles:
Instead of keeping your knowledge to yourself or letting it float around as though it were scholarship—and continuing to hang any of it solely

on classical poets and playwrights, or literature anyway (thus the literary staying so, and history or scholarship a sterile thing) why don't you commit yourself to some action in the area? Example situation Crete 1500 vis-a-vis Greek words mythology "future"—literature?

The problem with "Situation Crete 1500" as I saw it was the conspicuous absence there of any written poetry to work with, of any writing at all, in fact, except the so-called "Linear B" tablets. These clay tablets were inscriptions in an early form of Greek, indicating the names of gods and goddesses in whose temples grain and other supplies were stored. The poetry of Minoan Crete, as that of Homer, was presumably oral, and hasn't survived. Since I was interested in poetry, not archaeology, there was little in the Linear B tablets of interest to me.

Yet it was precisely this narrow sense of literature as something finished, written down, and wrapped up by specialist scholars for other specialist scholars, that you tried to bust in me and the other students in your class. You kept it at week after week as we listened to you construct the origins of Greek mythology, the origins of your own "myth and poetics" out of those barest of fragments of Second Millennium history that few of us knew anything about or were even convinced that we should know anything about. There was so little evidence, so much speculation. Wherever there was a shortage of facts on some question, your own imagination took over beautifully. It's funny, now, I suppose, but it seemed so mad then. I am amazed at how much I resisted. I was trying to write a serious paper on Euripides. I honestly thought that dissertations on Euripides were important contributions to literary scholarship.

You asked me to read a book about the Luvians, those obscure people of Asia Minor whose language may have directly influenced the development of the Cretan language. Cnossos, for example, the capital of ancient Crete, is a word formed of a man's name, "Cnos," with a Luvian genitive ending "–os." The word means "the city of Cnos" if one goes by the Luvian language. My assignment, after reading this book, was to reconstruct for you, as you put it, "the whole fucking Cretan language."

It was a task I didn't particularly want, even if I were capable of it, which I certainly was not. As I saw it, nothing more could be said on the subject than what G. L. Huxley, in his book, *Crete and the Luvians,* had already said. In fact, it struck me as absurd to even presume that there was more to be said than what Huxley's slim but exhaustive text offered.

But you kept bugging me. "When will you give us the Cretan language?" you kept demanding. "What do you have to do that's more important?"

I said there wasn't any Cretan language, and that I had no idea what you wanted me to do.

"Bullshit," you said, "of course there was."

You kept this up so much that I finally sent you a letter in which I said that while I didn't have any information on the Cretan language that you didn't already know, and that while I didn't believe any such information was to be found outside of Huxley's book, I would nonetheless do my best, and if that didn't satisfy you I would *invent* the Cretan language for you, and if *that* didn't satisfy you, I would (borrowing an Olsonism) "move my stick a little further down the beach" until I did.

That did it. You fired back the shortest note I ever received from you.

My dear Boer:

Move your stick right the hell off the beach
as far as I'm concerned.

Yours not at all,
Charles Olson

Of course, I never thought you would get so angry about it. As usual, I didn't realize how absolutely serious you were about everything. I guess I had thought of your badgering about the Luvians as a kind of educational game, and your preoccupation with the Second Millennium Greek world as only some kind of metaphor, nothing more, for handling a subject whose true area was elsewhere, which is to say, in the usual literary places.

I was wrong. It was no metaphor, and certainly no game. You really were living as a writer in a new world, the post-literary world of Cnossos at one pole and Maximus at the other.

At any rate your note shocked me as much as mine must have incensed you. I decided to call you up immediately and apologize. As soon as I identified myself on the phone, however, you said, "Phew, am I glad you called. I didn't want to go into that class tomorrow with anything like that hanging over our heads. Thanks for calling."

I had to approach the class, and you, with a new seriousness after that. While I never did get around to the Cretan language, I stopped resisting your claims for its importance.

After the death of your wife in the winter of 1964, you left Buffalo and returned to Gloucester, planning not to return at all for the spring semester. You sent me a letter, asking me to take over the class for you. The subject was still to be Crete, but you too had given up by then on the Luvians:

What I want you to do (in fact to improve your own situation on said orals) is to appear, as my leftenant, on Wednesday, if I am not at 3:20 P.M.—and initiate the work from that date to the May—date which etc. You need do no more than announce that the subject (for sd 13½ weeks, is to be, without interruption & as far as each can go, an island approximately directly south of the mainland of Crete—and *not* Sir Arthur etc. it is to be—nor Luvian either—the place very occupiable (in fact appear, please, with my *bronze mirror* which Charles Brover & his delightful & handsome wife, have on their bureau, & place that & each time return

with it in front of you—You are hereby asked, and requested, to con-
duct—look: the point of time carefully has not one thing to do with any
romantic or monotheistic aesthetic of—in fact that the so-called & assumed "kinks" of C-n-o-s-s-u-s
                    horshe-shit
had a *summer palace!*
ok?—and thereby, at least the 1st year, of your debt I, Charles Olson, shall
pay you (for retransfer to me at sd May date 1969)
                            ok?   love
                                O

   While the Buffalo English Department, at that time, was the
freest and most adventurous in the country, it was unfortunately
not about to have its graduate students teach its graduate courses.
They insisted that the course be dropped if you weren't going to
teach it yourself. So you returned, and resumed teaching, the ac-
tivity no doubt helping to ease the pain of Betty's loss. But after
that semester, you left for good.

Friendships came easy for you. Rapport was instantaneous,
whether because of your size, which never failed to impress a new-
comer, or the sheer charm and blarney of your speech. You had a
way of convincing people immediately that you were interested in
them.
   To young poets, who felt they belonged to an "underground"
that opposed literary "establishment," you appealed inevitably as a
great guru of myth and mysticism and as the leading "underground" poet. It mattered little that you claimed to detest mysticism and guru gimmickry. Or that you saw yourself as the main
line of American poetry after Pound and Williams. You *were* the
establishment.
   To graduate students, numbed by years of professional pedan-
try and aching with the academic blues, you were the paragon of

the antiacademic. A common Olson complaint, on the other hand, as you would pore over your dozens of Cambridge Ancient History pamphlets, was that academics and graduate students today weren't academic enough. They didn't know enough. They didn't read enough.

To housewives, faculty wives, student wives, lady poets, and lonely hearts everywhere, you presented yourself as a teddy bear with a heart of gold, to be hugged and nurtured, loved and fed.

To truck drivers and fishermen, waitresses and cleaning women, you were unfailingly an equal, a *compadre,* a man who would listen patiently to their own hard stories and who had a few of your own, who knew hard work and poverty firsthand and didn't have to patronize grief when he saw it. You valued their ability to get something done with their hands, though your own world—poetry!—was as far removed from theirs as the imagination could reach.

But you talked. And how you talked! You knew the words that everyone wanted to hear and had to hear. Who can say what you really were: a father in heaven? an honest-to-god prehistoric poet in the flesh in plastic fantastic America? a man who had all the answers? or should have? Whatever it was, you cherished the role. In fact, you insisted on it.

Once you told us how a former student of yours had come to Gloucester to see you, bringing his wife along, and how he started arguing with you about some point or other in one of your books.

"I had to put him down," you said, "and I hated to do it in front of his wife, but what does he expect when he comes down to lock horns with the big bull?"

And now the "big bull" was in Mansfield. You continued writing poems, the beginning of poems, notes on Connecticut history and other things, in the flaps of books, on the backs of envelopes, and on note pads:

the Blow is Creation
and the Twist the Nasturtium
is any one of Ourselves
And the place of it all?
    Mother Earth Alone

I prefer an earlier America. I didn't
know that I wd.

        And (a?) man,
I should think, would rather in fact like or
have liked the world they live in because
it is theirs if for no other reason
        than to

It was pasteurized 1st
which means of course the loss of
the pasture   and then it was
homogenized   which means of course
    the loss of man.

Nonetheless, one day things got so bad that, sadly, I had to throw you out of my house.

Let it be said that there is no one whose talk I ever enjoyed more than yours, Charles. It was so alive, so urgent—a nonstop basso profundo outpouring whose range could charm a kitten or stop a truck. God, it was exciting! I once even told you that so great was the power of your voice that if you told me to move to Nebraska or even to drop dead, I probably would have done it on the spot.

The days went on, after you were hired by the university, exactly as before. It became clear that you were encamped at my place for more than a few weeks' visit. There was nonetheless no let-up in your demand for attention. If anything, it increased. You would talk at table for hours, what seemed like days, with the same perfervid intensity. I held my classes for the required few hours each morning and came home to find you just getting up and ready for more uninterrupted talk. Sometimes it continued until dawn. I was able to get only two or three hours of sleep before my classes the next day.

It was a fascinating routine for the first few days, a bit repetitive after awhile, and then gradually exhausting. Finally, I couldn't listen anymore. It became impossible to keep up with you. Incredibly, it got to where I had to force myself to listen. I would remind myself that it was a privilege to have you, that there were others who would have given anything to hear you, that you were perhaps a lonely man and needed somebody to hear all this, that you had been too kind to me in the past not to be kind to you now and bear up. I tried every conceivable argument I could think of to keep awake and not drop asleep from weariness at the table. Then it got to where I couldn't even force that anymore. Your own vitality was unyielding. It wasn't human. Your own powers seemed to increase exactly as mine collapsed. I began to feel consumed by you—drained, devoured. Even the sound of your voice became oppressive. My head was aching. And though at times you seemed to be repeating yourself, I didn't even have the energy to speak up and tell you.

I no longer looked forward to coming home anymore, knowing that I would have to face another eighteen hours of it. But I thought, this is crazy, it's my house, it's my life, what the hell is going on? I told you how I felt, but when you started talking again it was hopeless. You were too shrewd at the game of words not to be able to handle my feeble pleas to ease up and lay off for awhile, a day even. And you would tell me not to be scared by it at all. "Don't be afraid," you would often interject, when you saw that my mind was more and more on what to do about you and not on what you were talking about. I realized that all this must have happened before, that with the extraordinary needs of your own mind, your own voice, your own heart's boundless passion for personal engagement, you had probably encountered others whose energies gave way too.

But tired and distracted, I was falling asleep on my job at the university. Once I even fell asleep at my desk there. Gradually I began to feel ill, and then even feverish. Yet the words kept coming from you, on and on out of some massive reservoir whose dam had burst.

When I would tell you outright that I was too weak for such long hours of talking like this day after day, you would tell me that I was stronger than you were and that that was why you had come to talk to me. And sometimes, when I would be falling asleep too obviously for you not to recognize it, I would tell you again that I was too weak for this and you would say, "I know you are and that's why I love you."

After it was definite that you would be working at the university, and it was obvious (at least to me) that you would have to find a house of your own, I brought home the newspapers every day hoping you would find some advertised rental. But while you gave them a few minutes' perfunctory attention, you never found anything that interested you. You seemed to give little thought to moving at all. I tried to impress upon you the urgency of getting your own place, that it would take time, though there were ample places to choose from, but you dismissed all efforts to select one for you and said not to worry, that you would get one sometime.

Finally, I told you that you would have to leave, if only for a day, because I was becoming ill and it was useless for you to go on like this when I just couldn't pay attention anymore and you were wasting your words on me. You told me again not to be afraid. But I told you it was not just a question of my being afraid, that I was sick. At this you said, "Whatever you got, I got double!" And then you went right on talking. Sometimes you made me laugh at what a master you were of getting your own way, and then you would laugh, too, at winning the game. What madness!

After days and days of this, you finally said okay—you would leave tomorrow for Gloucester, where you planned to return anyway to get your things to move down. The next day, however, the whole thing began again. You talked the entire day away just in saying goodbye, and then the night, too. You apologized, said you would leave the following day. When that day came, the same thing happened again.

At this point, I asked my friend and colleague, John Lobb, whom I had earlier introduced you to, to come home with me and help persuade you of the seriousness of the situation. I think I was by then delirious. I felt that nothing I said made any impression on you, or on anybody else for that matter. I had to invite someone else to present my case for me. It had all become that crazy. I had told other friends what was going on, that I was desperate for some rest, and asked endlessly for advice, but the whole situation seemed so zany to people that in most cases it only seemed to provoke amusement.

Lobb offered to talk to you, and when we arrived you were up and drinking coffee in the living room. You were in a jolly mood, but started in with a complaint that the telephone rang that morning and woke you up, so that you had not slept well. I went into the kitchen to make some coffee while Lobb stayed in the living room to talk to you.

He began by saying, as pointedly as possible, "Gee, Charles, I'm surprised to find you're still here. I thought you would have gone back to Gloucester by now to get your notes and stuff for your course.

"Notes?" you replied. "I don't need any notes! I've got them all, up here," pointing to your head. You were in such good spirits you started doing a dance for Lobb, an old Estruscan dance, you called it, with your palms extended in front and in back of you. I came back into the living room with the coffee.

When Lobb then explained to you that I was at the end of my rope, you stopped dancing. You said you were surprised at me for saying such a thing. I pleaded with you again that I was ill, had not slept for more than a few hours in days, and simply couldn't go on like this.

You told us abruptly that you would leave tomorrow. I reminded you that you had been saying that for days. You persisted though, and said you were entitled to another night because the telephone had disturbed your sleep that morning, that it was my telephone after all that had disturbed you, and that you weren't in the mood to go.

That was the last straw. I told you that the telephone was only an excuse and that if you didn't go I was going to. You said that was *fine,* that I *should* go. I told you it was my house and that I had a right to live in it. At that, you grabbed your cup of coffee and stormed out of the room, slamming the living room door shut on us as you went off to your room.

We sat there in dejected silence for awhile. We could hear you talking momentarily on the telephone in the kitchen. After about fifteen minutes of our trying to figure out what to do now, Lobb decided to go in and talk to you.

You were sitting on the enclosed porch off your bedroom, drinking coffee and reading the newspaper. Lobb asked if you wanted to go out to dinner and get something to eat. You said no, and told him that you wanted me to come back and see you, that you wanted to talk to me alone.

At the door I asked you if I could come in. You said yes, but didn't look up from your newspaper. Then you said, "What's the matter, Charlie, don't you love me anymore?"

"I do," I said, perhaps too craftily, under the circumstances, "but only according to my bond." You smiled.

I told you I was sorry, profoundly sorry, that it had come to this, that I was simply not strong enough to withstand the demands you were making, and that in any event I wanted you to know, before you left, that I was still your friend.

"Some friend!" you said, "sending me out into the cold to sleep in the streets!"

I told you I was not sending you out into the cold to sleep in the streets, that I had offered many times to get a room for you at a local inn, and furthermore, that it wasn't cold outside.

You said you were quite capable of getting your own rooms,

and "furthermore [deliberately mocking my own "furthermore"] I could have gone to any number of friends and they would have put me up for months if I wanted, and what's more, they have nicer furniture than you do."

I laughed at this last remark, but you didn't seem to mean it as a joke. "I didn't know you didn't like the furniture," I said, but it was silly, and obviously not the issue. I offered again to call for a room at the inn, but you said you had already called Bill Moynihan, my department head, who was driving out to pick you up, and you would be leaving my premises shortly. I said again that I hoped you were leaving as a friend.

You said nothing, kept looking at your newspaper, and I started to leave when you said, almost under your breath, "Fuck!"

I turned around and told you that wasn't fair, that I didn't want you to leave, in spite of all I had said, if you were going to leave feeling that way. You could have my house if you wanted it that much.

"You once told me," you said, "that you would even die for me if I told you to."

"No," I said, "I told you that I thought your voice was so overwhelming that if you told me to move to Nebraska or to drop dead I probably would have. That's not the same thing, and furthermore, I'm not ready to die for anybody, yourself included."

I started to leave. You said, simply, "Goodbye," and went on reading the newspaper. I left the house and went to the Lobbs' house, relieved that it was over. On the way to the Lobbs', I kept saying to myself those great lines of Martin Luther King: "Free at last, free at last, thank God in Heaven I'm free at last."

We went to a restaurant for dinner, and though I tried to get the memory of the last several days out of my head, I couldn't. I started wondering if Moynihan had taken care of you. At eight o'clock, I called Bill to find out how it went. His wife, Ruth, answered, and told me that there had been no rooms available at the Altnaveigh, the inn where I thought you would be going, or at the Willimantic Motor Inn, the only other hotel in the area. Everything was booked. She said the two of you had been gone for hours and were still out looking for a place. I told her that if you didn't find anything to have you come back to my house, and that I would spend the night with the Lobbs. At eleven, I phoned again, and she said that you did find a place, though she didn't know where, and that Bill had not returned yet. So I went home to bed and slept until noon. It may not have been the sleep of the just, but at that point I didn't care.

Moynihan told me later what had happened that night. He said that when you called him, you spoke in grave but excited tones: "I'm desperate and I need your help! I can't explain now but come out to the house within the hour and get me out of here!"

When Bill drove up, you were already coming out the door, your arms loaded with wicker baskets of clothes and things, saying, "Let's get the hell out of here. I can't stand this place!"

You left the door of the house wide open, however, and when Bill reminded you of this, you said, "Fuck the goddamn door!" So Bill himself got out of the car to close the door of the house, then noticed that *all* the doors of the house were wide open. As if to rid the place of a spirit, your spirit, you had propped open everything. Moynihan closed the doors and got back into the car. You were furious.

"It's a madhouse Boer's running in there," you said. "He needs to grow up. He's just a big baby, that's what he is! He's all fucked up with students running in and out all the time, the telephone never stops ringing, and I have to keep chasing them away!" Then you slammed your fist down on the dashboard and said, "Well, I don't need the bastard! I helped him more than he helped me. He'll come back to me again too, wait and see!"

The two of you drove off down Wormwood Hill Road on your way to the Altnaveigh, where you wanted to have dinner before anything else was to be decided. The ride calmed you down, and you started describing various landmarks to Bill along the way, especially the way the river ran parallel to the road. You knew where a liquor store was in the vicinity and gave directions to it. "I left all my equipment behind," you said, ominously, "and I need to pick up some supplies."

When you got to the liquor store you charged in, Moynihan said, like Pancho Villa, and bought two bottles of Cutty Sark. After you paid for them, you gave one bottle to Bill, saying, "I don't need *two!*"

When you finally arrived at the Altnaveigh, it was packed with students and parents of students. There were no rooms available, so Moynihan offered to put you up at his house, or at one of several other faculty homes, but you absolutely refused, saying you would only stay "in a public place," and that you wanted to be on your own.

You sat down to dinner at the restaurant. When you heard the Montreal accent of the waitress, Germaine Girouard, you started in immediately on how charming she was, how healthy the sex life was in Catholic Mediterranean countries, and what a great waitress she was. After a while, over a steak, you started calling for her, when you would be in another part of the restaurant, by snapping your fingers and yelling "Frenchie!"

Moynihan, shocked, lowered his voice and said, "Charles, you can't talk to her that way."

"God, if I haven't earned the right to talk the way I want, nobody has!" you replied.

When it became apparent to Bill it was going to be a long night, and that he might have to drive you to Hartford for a hotel room, or even back to Gloucester, he decided to call Jack Davis. Davis, whom you called "Jake," had met you at my house on the day you were interviewed. Afterwards, he told me you were "the most interesting human being" he had ever met.

Moynihan told Davis the whole story on the phone, how he needed his help, and said, jokingly, but no doubt a bit desperate himself now, "Jack, get off your ass and earn your pay!" So Davis came and joined you.

They told you they would take you to a hotel in Hartford, but by this time you had decided that you were going to stay at the Altnaveigh and nowhere else. You called Germaine over and asked again if there weren't any available rooms upstairs. When she said no, and informed you again that everything was taken for the night, you asked for the owner of the place. When the owner, Fred Haddad (whom you would come to address later on as "Mister Fred"), came over to the table, you said, "I know how you guys operate. You've got a couple of rooms in back up there, don't you, that are always empty. Give me one of them!"

But the owner said no, he was very sorry, there were no rooms in back or anywhere else that were available, there was just no room. At this you got up out of your seat and shouted, "Well, make room!"

"Mister Fred" thought it over and said that he could give you a room that he had in the nearby town of Willimantic, but only if you were really desperate, because it was not much of a room. At this you rejoiced, and said, "I can stay anyplace so long as it's public!" So you paid four dollars for the room and started to go.

You took a dish of rolls off the table, and other things that were left over, and scooped them into one of your wicker baskets. The three of you left for Willimantic.

Germaine had given you directions, and you found the place without any difficulty. It was located over a bar, in the center of town. You went up the stairs and found the room, to your surprise, unlocked. There was nothing in it except a bed, and the bed was tiny. The walls were made of plasterboard, as if the room were only some small extension of something else. There was nowhere to sit down in the room, no chairs, so you all sat down on the bed.

"This is a hell of a place to leave you," Moynihan said. "It's like a scene from a B-movie. At least let us drive you to Hartford and put you up in a good hotel."

"No," you said, "it's clean, and these are my kind of people here.

This is my kind of place. And you know what I'm talking about, Bill, coming from Haverhill." (Willimantic, an impoverished mill town and home of the American Thread Company, is known as "Thread City" to its inhabitants.)

"How can you even sleep in that bed?" they asked you. "It's too small for you."

"I'll take it apart," you said gamely.

So the three of you sat there, talking until midnight, passing the Cutty Sark around to be sipped from the bottle. Every so often you would interject quotations from *King Lear* that were now increasingly appropriate. Then Moynihan and Davis said good night, and left.

The next day, early in the afternoon, I was taking out a bag of trash when suddenly a big white car came flying up the long driveway, screeching and skidding, and then hitting the side of the porch and scraping it. "Oh no," I said, "it's him!"

You jumped out of the car, beaming a huge grin at me, and said, "Cholly, how are ya? You're looking better today."

I didn't know what to say. I asked you whose car this was, since it now sported a scraped fender.

"Don't worry," you said, "I can get another one."

I asked you how your night was, and you said it was "crazy, but all right." You wanted me to sit down with you on the grass to talk, but I was shivering, still slightly feverish. You said the sun would do us both some good. It was so encouraging to know that you weren't still angry, or didn't appear so, that I decided to sit down with you on the grass sick or not. We sat there a few minutes while you told me the grim details of your night in "Thread City." The bed had collapsed during the night and you were up at six because trucks kept roaring down the street all night waking you up.

While you were telling me this, Peter and Paul Kugler came

over, and they listened too. Paul recognized the room as one he had himself only recently lived in. And the bed was originally broken by him, so that he had placed cardboard and a dresser drawer under to keep it propped up, and not to have to pay for it when he moved out. After he moved out, nobody, apparently, would rent it, because it was so dismal, and the bed remained propped that way until you took it.

You burst out laughing at the coincidence (you preferred to call it a "concordance") and the two of you continued laughing as you compared rhapsodic views of Willimantic. Both of you thought of the town as a great, if horrible, experience.

I asked you again how you got the car, a new Plymouth Fury. You said you rented it from Avis in Willimantic that morning. I reminded you that you didn't have a license. Was Avis trying that hard? You said you simply talked a little to the kid who was on duty, who was "hip."

"You know how I do it," you said, "a little sweet-talking did it."

By this time I was shivering visibly, and had stomach cramps. I told you we should go into the house.

"Oh no," you said, "I wouldn't think of it. I know how you feel."

I told you it would be an honor to have you come into my house again, and with only a little further hesitation, you came in. You acted as if you were coming in for the first time and waited to be told to sit down. How formal you could be! I was relieved that you didn't appear angry about your eviction of the day before.

There was still a bit of reluctance, however, on the part of both of us, as to whether the whole affair was to be so easily dropped. You were obviously hurt, even if you didn't show it. We talked about trivial business for awhile. Then, in the kitchen, it came out. You looked at me for a minute before your spoke.

"I want to tell you something, Cholly, and never you forget it:

Never shove the one who loves you. Never shove the one who loves you."
And then, to emphasize your point, you started shoving me around the floor, as you repeated the words, playfully, but firmly, until I was shoved up against the refrigerator door and couldn't be shoved any more. Then, punctuating each word with a mild jab to my stomach, you said again, *"Never-shove-the-one-who-loves-you."*

I said I wouldn't.

We went on for awhile talking about possible houses for you in the Eastford area that you would be passing through on your way back to Gloucester that afternoon. After coffee, you left again, very excited about driving, which you liked to do. We walked out with you to the car where you showed us with a kind of pride all the dials and gadgets on the dashboard. Then, after turning on the radio, you sped off to Gloucester, screeching and skidding on the driveway gravel as fast as you had driven in.

You returned in the middle of the week and booked a room at the Altnaveigh. You planned to rent a house, and started making serious inquiries, though nothing seemed to materialize. One place, however, drew your eye, and you drove out to examine it in person. It had sixteen rooms, five fireplaces, a terrace, a stable, an outdoor pool, an indoor heated pool, and a sauna. It was being restored by an Italian family, who came on weekends to finish it. The only drawback in renting it was that the whole family—brothers, cousins, nephews, uncles—lived there every weekend they worked on it. When you asked them how many more weekends that would be, they said, "A couple of years maybe." You decided not to take it.

The Altnaveigh now became your permanent quarters. You came to love the staff there, and they became very fond of you. At one point you were even inquiring if you could buy the place and continue living there with the entire staff of an inn at your command.

In the restaurant downstairs, we would spend many nights over dinner, where you talked of American history, Greek poets, the "real" William Carlos Williams, and all the other topics that previously I could only listen to in a sleepless daze. It was a lot easier talking to you at your own table. The pace, dictated more now by the hours of the restaurant than by your own metabolism, was a lot less driven.

We talked a lot about Williams. I had mentioned the fact that in my poetry course I always discussed *The Maximus Poems* directly after *Paterson*. *Paterson,* the great American poem in praise of the local, was a lead-in. You went crazy!

"I got nothing out of *Paterson,* you said. "I owe that Bill Williams *nothing.*"

You mentioned the time you went to call on Dr. and Mrs. Williams in Rutherford, shortly after you had published, in *Mayan Letters,* a brief critique of Pound and Williams on epic. After a friendly dinner, Williams and you went into the library. Williams quietly pulled down from the shelf his copy of *Mayan Letters,* opened it to the critical passage, and asked you, sternly, "What do you *mean* by this?"

You didn't know what to say. You hadn't expected this sudden rebuke after such a pleasant dinner. Then, when Williams went out of the room, Flossie came in, and, for lack of anything better to say, you told her that her husband was "the greatest short story writer in the world, including any Russians." Your evening at the Williams' was not a success.

But you really meant what you said to her, you told me. Williams was a great short story writer; that is what he was, not a poet. You said he acquired this gift simply from talking to all the Polish women who came into his office. "He just wrote down everything they told him. Everything. Imagine!"

The best poem that Williams ever wrote, you said, and the most telling one, was "The High Bridge on the Tagus River at Toledo." In this poem, Williams tells how he tried to cross a Spanish bridge but a shepherd was crossing with his sheep at the same time, and Williams had to give way as the sheep passed him. As a poet, Williams was "bemused," you said, by this experience.

"And this is just where Williams shows his failure to understand cities. In Spain, men know to give way to sheep. Williams didn't realize that. And he didn't realize that all cities are one. The city was a structure that lasted through time—and by confining himself to the local Williams failed to realize what was wrong with the city. It was," you said, "the error of the local."

On another occasion, you mentioned your poetry reading at the Queen Elizabeth Hall in London in 1966. A number of internationally known poets were invited and the place was packed. You seemed to think of the event as a kind of contest to determine the world's best poet. You were personally impressed with the Italian poet Giuseppe Ungaretti. Ungaretti, you said, stole the show.

"He was marvelous. He's just a little guy but the words just kiss out of him." And you demonstrated for me exactly what you meant by putting your hand to your lips and kissing out the Italian word, "mare." "Ma-re, il mare, il maah-re, il maaaah-re. Imagine an American poet getting away with something like that! Just that same word like that! Only the Italians can do it, and believe you me, Ungaretti did!"

I said I didn't think Italian poets had such a monopoly on that kind of thing, and I recited some lines from Williams' poem, "The Catholic Bells":

> Ring ring ring ring ring ring ring
> Catholic Bells—!

You laughed. "Who wrote that?" you asked.
"Williams," I said.
"No! What's it called?"
"The Catholic Bells," I said.

You seemed astounded. "Did Bill Williams really write that?" you asked incredulously. "Are you sure Bill Williams wrote that?"

You were much more respectful towards Pound than Williams. In Gloucester, once, you inscribed for me a copy of Pound's *Drafts and Fragments,* which had just come out and which you had two copies of. You were particularly impressed with the lines:

> Many errors,
> a little rightness,
> to excuse his hell,
> and my paradiso.

You called my attention to this several times. You were moved by Pound's reference here to Dante, you said, "as if Dante only wrote an *Inferno,* while Pound wrote a *Paradiso.* Imagine the nerve! When Pound can say something like 'paradiso terrestre,' however, you can see where Pound and I are related as poets."

Shortly after this, you sent me the following note:

It suddenly dawned on me just after you left that of course Ezra does mean his hell and 'my' inferno—that is no old anything like monkey business but like earth to earth—(Like he told me once, with a discomfort I felt then and still can hear, how reluctantly often he'd have to accept Yeats' pressing on him, at Rapallo, to be a 4th at ouija board!

Charles Olson meets Ezra Pound for the first time on January 4, 1946, at St. Elizabeth's Hospital in Washington, where Pound is held pending his trial for treason. Dorothy Norman had invited Olson in November of the previous year to cover the Pound trial as a reporter for her magazine, *Twice-a-Year.* Olson's first view of Pound is at the initial arraignment. He is struck by the pitiful spectre of the man, "grey and alone," in a democratic court of law "so alien to Pound's elitism." When Olson finally meets Pound in the hospital, he decides to keep a journal of this and subsequent visits.

Pound asks him, when he is introduced, "Is it possible I have seen your name on something in print?"

Olson thinks this a "neat" way to begin. But it is a difficult relationship and Olson feels qualms and doubts about continuing his visits as Pound keeps interjecting bits of anti-Semitism into the conversation. After several months, Olson feels free enough to criticize Pound for thinking he could "traffic with snobs and bastards and get away with it."

He feels that no really close friendship with Pound is possible because Pound is "a politician of friendship." One day Pound spends some time praising the fanatical right-wing columnist, Westbrook Pelger. Olson writes later that night:

For the first time the full shock of what a fascist s.o.b. Pound is caught up with me. I guess I had to feel it on my own America before I could have a realization. For Pegler I have traveled through and understand. Pound's praise of him reveals his utter incomprehension of what is going on. I wondered then how long more I can hold out my hand to him as a poet and a man. I suppose I shall tell him one day I am the son of immigrants, this influx of second class citizens whom Pegler and Pound think has made impure their Yankee America of pioneers and Biddles. That my father was killed fighting for the right of labor men to organize in unions. That decadent democracy gave me the chance to grope out of the American city into some understanding of what life is, and how to peg a smart fascist s.o.b. like Pegler—and Ezra Pound. Meanwhile I shall do what I can, as long as I can, for this fool of hate because once he was also a fool of love.

Dorothy Pound tells him that Ezra finds the visits stimulating. Gradually, a better relationship evolves with "the politician of friendship." Pound, desperate for what he calls "15 minutes *sane* conversation daily," later writes to his lawyer that "Olson saved my life."

After St. Elizabeth's, Olson doesn't see Pound again until 1965, when both poets are invited to read at "The Festival of Two Worlds" in Spoleto. They meet in the theater where the poetry readings are given. Pound stands in a balcony of honor overlooking the stage "like an Umbrian angel," Olson describes it later. Olson stands below, looking up at him, his hands barely reaching the bottom of the balcony. Pound looks down and talks to him, "standing for a time on my fingertips."

Though critical of Pound's politics, your conversations on poetry often emphasized the need for poets to be political. Dryden was more important than Pope, you said, because he was close to the throne. You disliked all poetry of an epicene nature, "like Pope's." "They write that way because they don't have any real power," you said.

One day you were talking to my neighbor, Tom Meddick, about your father. You said you didn't like being an only child and that you really had five fathers: Wilbert Snow, your favorite teacher at Wesleyan; Lou Douglas, a Gloucester fisherman and "the hero of my poem"; your real father; Ezra Pound; and Carl Sauer, the geographer. You were exuberant that you had talked, by phone, with two of your "fathers" in the last few days (Snow and Sauer).

We talked of Sauer's work, which had been of continuing interest to you for years. Sauer's writings on Mexico were required preparatory reading for your own *Mayan Letters;* his writings on the end of the Ice Age were the scientific source for your interest in that period and the basis for your post-Laurentian pamphlet, *Pleistocene.* His seminal writings on "The Morphology of Landscape" provided an important apparatus for your stance toward Gloucester in *The Maximus Poems.* And you said you had taken three poems "already" from Sauer's recent book about early expeditions to America, *Northern Mists*. "It's a gold mine," you said. Though you admired Sauer's prose for its own sake, you hadn't read *The Early Spanish Main* "because I never could get interested in the Caribbean."

You told me about the phone call to Sauer, how nervous you were to call up your old mentor, who was now 80, and to whom you hadn't spoken in twenty years.

"I felt like a fucking bride when the phone was ringing," you said. When he answered, you blared out, "This is Charles Olson!"

Sauer replied, "Oh yes, Charles, how are you?"

"Imagine," you told me later, "after twenty years, just like that!"

I once teased you about your own role as father figure to so many dozens, perhaps hundreds, of young (and some quite old) people, how you seemed to relish and encourage the role though always with a modest demurral. One day when you were calling Pound one of your five "fathers," I said, "I guess that makes Pound my grandfather."

"Don't tell me you think of me as a father figure too?" you asked.

"Of course," I replied. "One only has to meet you to feel adopted."

"Well, you're wrong," you said. "You're more like my own real father than anyone I've ever met. I'm *your* son!"

Olson's father, Carl Olson, is a postman in Worcester, Massachusetts, for most of his life. He is a gentle and friendly man who chats with everyone along his delivery route, romps with everybody's dog, and brings home little surprises every day for his son.

He attempts to unionize the postal workers in Worcester and is hated for it. His bosses go out of their way to make things difficult for him. They remove him from his lifelong route, cut his pay, and hound him with inspectors who follow him daily looking for mistakes. It is this harassment, Olson says later, that leads to his death in 1935 of a cerebral hemorrhage.

That summer, he is about to leave for a postal convention in Cleveland, which he has long been looking forward to and making plans for. He asks his son if he can borrow his suitcase, which is bigger and newer than his own, in order to make a good impression on everyone at the convention. His son refuses, saying he wants it himself for the following weekend. The father becomes angry, but says nothing more. A few days later he has a stroke, and on the way to the hospital, though he speaks to his wife, he says no more to his son. This angry silence endures to his death.

Olson writes a story about his father called, "The Post Office," describing the ordeal that leads to his death. He never publishes it.

Often the conversations at these Altnaveigh suppers would center around books we were reading. There was a book you had read for every conceivable subject that came up. When I would mention Stonehenge, for example, you would immediately ask if I had read *Stonehenge Decoded*. I hadn't, but I told you of visiting Stonehenge the year before, and how the British government had put up a small barbed wire fence around the borders, because some students from London had gone in one night and indelibly painted some of the stones with political slogans. You were outraged that the fence had been put up and said it should come down.

"Don't you think they should protect the place from vandals?" I asked, rather amazed at your attitude.

You hesitated, then agreed with me, but just as suddenly you changed your mind again. "No, goddamn it! Keep it open! Get Druids for guards if you have to, but keep it open!"

"What we learn from Jung is that you have to let words swim into our soul."

"There are no thinkers in America," you kept saying. "I'm the only thinker in America. There are no intellectuals in this country. When *Time* magazine did that article on intellectuals in America, they quoted Lawrence Ferlinghetti and LeRoi Jones! Imagine! Larry's a sweet guy and all that—but really!"

All your life, you said, you had been "mapping."

"I have only five more miles to go, five more miles and my map will be complete."

Though your "map" in this case meant something very special, I had found you that evening upstairs in your room at the Altnaveigh, where you had just been sent a couple of Geodesic Survey maps of Mansfield and Windham County. The maps were enormous. We rolled them out until they covered the entire floor of your room. Then we crawled over them, looking for various roads or places that, for one reason or another, you had become interested in. The maps were so crisp that every time we examined a road in one corner, the other end would start to roll up until you had to crawl over to that corner to hold it down. On your way over to that corner, however, another important road would catch your attention and you would call me over to see it. Then my corner would roll up and we'd have to start all over again.

"Shit," you'd grumble, or something equally expressive, and crawl on.

I asked you about the last poem in the recently published *Maximus IV, V, VI,* about your setting out now "in a box upon the sea." Was this the end of *The Maximus Poems?* Were you finished?

"No," you said, "you don't understand that. Don't you realize that *all* my books end with an image of the vehicular?"

"There are four legs to stand on," you said. "The first, be romantic. The second, be passionate. The third, be imaginative. And the fourth, never be rushed."

Shortly before this, Jack Kerouac had died, and you were deeply affected by it. You were startled that he had died so young. You considered attending the funeral, though you gave up the idea when you couldn't find out whether he would be buried in Florida or Massachusetts.

I asked you about Kerouac and you told me of a strange meeting you had with him only a few years before. You said that Kerouac had come to Gloucester to see you one Sunday night, and when he arrived at the back steps to your second-floor apartment, he shouted up to you, "Olson, the red carpet please! Get out the red carpet!"

You said that of course you didn't have any red carpet to put down for him but you took what you considered to be the next best thing, the Sunday newspaper, and carefully placed a page on each step down the back stairs. Kerouac was pleased at the gesture, especially when he found, going up the stairs, that one of the pages he was walking on contained an article on him, with his picture.

The evenings we met for dinner, especially those after your weekly class, became a ritual after a while. Students had told me that you would end the class punctually (which you never did in Buffalo, often going on for hours overtime) by saying, "I have to leave now, I have a very important dinner engagement." You took these dinners as serious occasions. Under no circumstances was I to miss them.

One day, however, I was ill again (it was the worst season for illness in my life) and had been home in bed after getting an antibiotic shot at the hospital. I telephoned the English Department office to have the secretary tell you that I couldn't meet you that night for our usual dinner. At four o'clock, however, she called me back to say that Mr. Olson said to tell me that I'd better be there and no excuses. I asked her if I could speak to you, but in the background I could hear you fuming at her that you weren't going to speak to me "over no phone!"

I didn't realize you would get so angry about it, and I certainly didn't want to revive the wrath that had been released by my earlier "shoving" of you. After an hour of feeling even worse for disappointing you, I decided to send a student in to your classroom, when you were finished, to tell you that I would meet you as usual.

The student waited outside your classroom door until everyone left. He walked up to you and asked, somewhat coyly, "Would you like to have dinner at the Altnaveigh tonight?"

"Well I'm glad somebody wants to have dinner with me," you replied.

When he proceeded to tell you that I would come, and that I was reluctant at first because I had just been given an antibiotic shot and wasn't feeling well, it amused you.

"Boer's been out friggin' with the horses again!" you exclaimed.

When we finally sat down to dinner that night at the Altnaveigh, I was soaking wet with fever.

You said, "Why are you sweating so much? That's not like you, Cholly."

You seemed delighted, however, to see me, and launched in upon a thousand stored-up topics, none of which I could even vaguely follow. I was unable to eat anything. After a while, you said, "Cholly, what's the matter, you really sick?"

When I explained again that I was, you became very concerned, and told me to go home and go to bed, that I shouldn't be out.

I was about to leave, when I found out that for some reason you had failed to make your usual reservation at the Altnaveigh for that night, having just returned from Gloucester. Once again there were no rooms available. I invited you to come back out to my house for the night, adding that I would have to go to bed immediately anyway.

At first you said you wouldn't think of it, the way I was feeling. But I assured you that it would be okay, that I would go to bed immediately and probably wouldn't even know you were there. You still refused, said you wouldn't think of it. No longer able to argue, I told you then where there was another hotel, and started to go. Suddenly you said, hesitating for a second, "Well, if you're sure it wouldn't be any trouble?"

I assured you it wouldn't be any trouble, that I would go directly to bed. You still hesitated but finally we left.

Since I was sick, you insisted that we drive out in your Plymouth Fury, which by now you were quite fond of; so fond, in fact, that you never got around to returning it. You kept the car, without notifying the company, for nearly three months, though you were supposed to return it the day after you rented it.

Pulling out of the driveway of the inn, I told you to make a left turn, but you just as quickly told me not to tell you directions, that you would find my house, you would take care of everything, I was in good hands. I was to tell you only if you made a wrong turn. You made two wrong turns.

You kept talking all the way back to the house, slowing the car down almost to a stop at times as if you forgot you were driving. After we got out of the car, you stood in the driveway, looking up at the stars, talking about "the great and wonderful condition of the solstice tonight," until I, shivering, made a dash for the door.

When we got in, I quickly made up a bed for you, then went into my room. You followed me in and continued talking for at least another two hours, until you realized how late it was getting.

"There I go again," you said, 'and I promised you could go right to bed. Well, it just goes to show you, doesn't it?"

One day, while you were getting a cup of coffee in the Humanities Building, one of your graduate students, Bernard Horn, came in. You asked him what he was doing, what was he into? Horn replied that he had started to write some poems.

You had always maintained a reluctant stance toward reading manuscripts of students' verse and your approach was to tell students to show you their poems when they were published, not before.

Several students in your class had not come that day and had gone instead to Stephen Spender's house to read their poems. Spender, who had been serving as Writer-in-Residence at the university for two years, was holding weekly gatherings at his house for student poets. The idea was to create an opportunity for them to read their poems and hear criticism from each other. You didn't like that at all! You said you were opposed to people reading their poems in public to each other. You were even more opposed to such people calling themselves "poets." You said they should simply describe themselves as "writing poems," as Horn had just said of himself. And if they did have to recite poems in public, you preferred that they recite the poems of others, not themselves.

You told Horn that when you were in Vancouver one day, walking down the corridors of the university, somebody in a classroom drew you in with a question about Wordsworth's "Prelude." You proceeded to talk to the class about the poem. But over lunch that day, you said, Allen Ginsberg surprised and "defeated" everybody by getting up and reciting that part of "The Prelude" which you had yourself just been talking about.

"That's what you have to do," you said.

On the days you taught your seminar you managed to encounter very few members of the faculty. You had an office but never used it. Part of your motive for changing the hour the class met, from four in the afternoon to eight at night, was to avoid even further any random contact with the faculty. In part this attitude was due to the usual antiacademic stance of your poetic generation—never look like you're one of *them*—and if it was a kind of intellectual arrogance, which it certainly was, it was also due to an increasing resistance you felt toward any casual socializing.

You were always ready to extend yourself in conversation with persons who offered some natural intensity in their lives that you could pry open and enjoy. Of these, waitresses, nurses, and postmen seemed perhaps more promising than English professors. You made a point of always telling people, "I don't socialize, I personalize."

You felt that the kind of academics you did like, the kind you could *use,* were becoming extinct. You had the greatest respect for those-old-fashioned men of scholarship who knew their subject well enough to answer a learned inquiry with authority. But where were they these days? Professors had become "hip," nice guys, had acceded to students' demands for entertainers—an exaggerated view perhaps, but in your eyes they were all akin to a gang of hired guns who couldn't even shoot.

"Nobody *knows* anything anymore," you would moan, whenever you had trouble tracking down some date or fact.

One day you went to your mailbox in the English Department office late in the afternoon. No one was there. While you were reading the mail, however, Lee Jacobus, an assistant professor of English, came in. Jacobus walked up to you and politely introduced himself. You looked him over a second and asked, gruffly, "And what do *you* teach?"

"Milton," he replied.

"Well *you*, sir, at least have a subject!"

One day I found you very depressed. You said you had tried to make a date to go to the movies with a girl from your seminar. She had already seen the film, so she told you to go to it and she would meet you for a drink later at a local bar. You took your time, as usual, in getting to the bar afterwards and when you got there the bartender told you that she had waited an hour for you and left.

There you were, Charles—passionate, romantic, and certainly imaginative—but you should have rushed.

As you continued your tenure at the Altnaveigh, its staff became increasingly considerate towards you. You usually stayed in your room during the early evening when dinner was being served downstairs. Then, about nine o'clock, you would come to the top of the stairs, naked except for a sheet you clutched onto, and yell down: "Germaine! Is everybody gone?"

Germaine would then come up carrying food to your room, or if everybody was gone, she would tell you to come down and you'd go to the kitchen, wrapped in your sheet, for supper. Often, when there were still many people downstairs, your voice from the top of the stairs could be heard booming throughout the restaurant: "Germaine! Germaine!"

After a while, they asked you to be more discreet. Since there were no telephones in the rooms, you would creep out into the hall, clutching the sheet, and use the pay phone in the hallway to call down to the kitchen to tell them to send something up. The inn of course never served customers in their rooms before Charles Olson came. But it didn't take very long before an exception was made for you.

"You know how I do it," you would say, whenever I expressed astonishment at how you continually managed to get people to do things for you that weren't done for anyone else. "You just gotta ask!"

On those nights when you planned to come down to dinner formally, and always on class nights, I joined you. The Altnaveigh is a delightful place in many ways but one of its unique advantages is the absence of Muzak or other synthetic merriment to numb the diners. On the other hand, it's a restaurant frequented by the parents of students when they visit the university. It's not unusual to find several such families at the various tables sitting in a kind of embarrassed silence, the father perhaps wondering if his son has been swayed by the Commie professors yet, the mother wondering if her daughter is telling her everything, the kids hoping their parents won't make too bad an impression on the inevitable roommate the parents have invited along. Most of the time the only sound one can hear is that of knife and fork at the next table, where people are eating in a similar embarrassed silence. The absence of musical sound-control only seems to magnify the self-consciousness of these good New England families.

Thus, Charles, when you would be talking, elaborating with delicious gestures and table-poundings the endless points of your own ebullient stories, heads would turn, fathers would peer out from under the lower halves of their Benjamin Franklin glasses. "Who's *he*?" one could hear muttered in the distance.

Your size, of course, always grabbed them too. One little old lady once even had the temerity to come over to our table and ask you to stand up so that she could see how tall you were. Without stopping your story for an instant, or even looking at her, you quickly stood up, then just as quickly sat down again as she squealed with delight.

Nor was all this lurking interest in your person peculiar to the Altnaveigh. One night in Gloucester, when we went to dinner at the Surf Restaurant, we passed a table on the way to our own where I heard a voice say, "Now there he is again. Who is he?"

The Surf Restaurant is located on the city boundary between Gloucester and Magnolia. You deliberately used to sit on the Magnolia side, you said, "Because if I'm in Gloucester I'm working, and I'd have to spend the night pumping the waitresses for news."

We had a long wait for our table that night, at least an hour, and you became worried that the Surf didn't want to serve us.

"We might not get served at all," you said, "because once I brought 'The Fugs' here and I don't think the restaurant liked it."

I said that if they didn't serve us I was personally going to serenade them with a chorus from "Slum Goddess of the Lower East Side." Fortunately it never came to that. We did get served, and in fact were the last ones to leave. They interrupted our conversation at midnight and asked that we pay the check.

Outside the restaurant, we went for a short walk on the beach. You wanted to point out "the boundary stone of Gloucester," a herm-like marker that divided the Magnolia shore from Gloucester's.

"Sit on it," you said. "Sit on it and feel the energy. Do you feel it?"

I felt nothing but a cold pointed stone sticking me in the ass.

Nonetheless, looking at the sea, and sitting on the boundary stone of Gloucester, I made up a quick poem in French about boundaries and recited it for you:

> La mer
> est
> la mére
> de nous
> tous.

You laughed and said it was like a poem you were working on, which you recited, slowly and even hesitantly, as if each word contained a sentence unsaid:

> The moon . . .
> the mother . . .
> and the child

In a conversation with Paul Kugler one day, you said that every young person should be exposed to the writings of Thornton Burgess. You told him he didn't have the right kind of childhood if he hadn't read Thornton Burgess.

"What do you mean?" Paul said. "My mother read us every Burgess book that was ever written, and she even knew 'Aunt Sally' personally."

When he went on to tell you how he had grown up on Cape Cod near the house, "the briar patch," "the laughing brook," and the "golden meadow" where Burgess' Aunt Sally lived, it was too good to be true. You wanted to meet his mother, Lee Kugler, immediately.

You phoned her in Boston, where she now lived, and told her, mysteriously, she was, for you, the statue in *The Winter's Tale*.

"What do you mean?" she asked.

"You read the play and you'll know what I mean," you replied.

Intrigued, she decided to come down to Mansfield, where she met you at the Altnaveigh. You immediately started pumping her for everything she knew about Aunt Sally.

Aunt Sally, no relation to Burgess, was a former nurse who had worked with psychiatric patients. Deciding after a while that she hated people and really loved animals, she became a recluse in Sandwich, Massachusetts, where her house and property soon became an animal kingdom. She had trapdoors built into her kitchen for raccoons, squirrels, and other animals to come and go as they pleased. Thornton Burgess heard of her and decided to pay a visit. He spent the entire night with her, taking pictures until dawn of all the animals that came to call. He was so moved by this woman's devotion to animals that he set up a special fund to take care of her. She inspired many of his stories and he finally wrote an account of her, *Aunt Sally and Her Friends*.

After she died, the animals continued to come for years, looking for their Aunt Sally. Her house was later turned into a gift shop in Sandwich called The Country Mouse.

Listening to Lee Kugler's firsthand account of this woman, you were fascinated. You had no idea, you said, that Aunt Sally was a real person, and you promptly borrowed her copy of *Aunt Sally and Her Friends.*

You told her how you had been trying for years to get the original editions of Burgess' books, with Hamilton Cady's illustrations. Burgess had lived in Gloucester and his work was therefore fair game for Gloucester's epic poet.

You said you once went to see Cady, who also had a house in Gloucester, but it was a disappointing experience. Cady was 89, and too old to talk. You had gone there chiefly to look out the windows and observe the scenery from which Cady had drawn his illustrations. Instead, all you could see was "a horrible green" in Cady's kitchen that spoiled your whole impression of the place.

I should comment here, Charles, on how sensitive you were to landscapes—especially Gloucester landscapes. You would often pause for long periods outdoors to stare at things—a sunset, a tree, the angle of a stone wall, the location of an old house, and of course the sea, the omnipresent Gloucester sea. You walked slowly, so slowly that it could take an hour sometimes just to get across a road. You called yourself "the last walker in America." And you described what you saw with a painter's precision rather than a poet's license. A great admirer of the nineteenth-century Gloucester painter, Fitz Hugh Lane, you often compared his panoramic canvases of the harbor and Cape Ann with your own work as Gloucester's poet. Two American landscape artists, a century apart.

Lee Kugler and you became good friends. Since you were so interested in Thornton Burgess, she made the mistake of telling you how avidly she used to read Joseph C. Lincoln's books too.

"I did likewise when I needed that sentimental shit," you said.

One of the waitresses at the Altnaveigh, Blanche Adams, was a student in the English Department at the university. By "concordance" she was also a friend of the Brovers. She had been to their house shortly after you smashed their glass table. Although the Brovers had told her about you, she didn't realize you were now staying at the Altnaveigh.

One day when she was on duty and saw you sitting at a table, she decided to introduce herself. She assumed it was you, she said later, by your "size and power." She walked over and said, "Are you Charles Olson? I heard you were in town because I saw the Brovers' table."

"That's a funny way to find out I'm in town," you replied.

Blanche had heard Robert Creeley and Robert Duncan read their poetry at a conference in Boulder, Colorado. She told you how much she "dug" the performances and you agreed that that was what it was all about—performance. When she asked why you didn't read at the Boulder Conference, you told her that you weren't as famous as Creeley and Duncan.

"Are *you* a performer?" she asked. You thought about it for a minute and decided you were.

Blanche found it "beautiful" to watch you eat. You'd tell her what each dish tasted like, and would order each course several times if you liked it. You always ordered dinner in several steps, trying everything at least once before ordering the next.

She sat at the table with you as you ate, as the other waitresses often did. You asked her how she felt about being a waitress. When she replied that she liked it, you advised her not to go on to graduate school in English. "Keep waiting," you said.

When Blanche told you that she too wrote poetry, but never showed her poems to anyone, you said she should go ahead and show them. "they're *for* people, you know."

One day she found you sitting at a peculiar angle at the table and asked you about it. You said you were sitting there because you wanted to see a certain tree out the window in the yard, and that you wanted very much to be able to walk on the top of that tree. For days, thereafter, she said, you sat at that same table, and your conversation would come back frequently to the idea of walking on the tops of trees.

I suspect you got the idea of walking on the tops of trees from a passage in Carlos Castaneda's book, *The Teachings of Don Juan*, that extraordinary account of the relationship between the author, a graduate student in anthropology, and Don Juan, an aged Yaqui Indian from Sonora, Mexico. You were very fond of the book, and had recommended it to many people in recent months. You even cited passages from it to your class.

"Castaneda's been working with Don Juan," you told them, as they dutifully wrote it all down, "and he's been doing very well on the drugs. Don Juan comes to him and says, 'You're ready now for this' and hits him with it. And he says, 'But you have to be very careful with this one, it's dangerous. It can take you over. It can destroy you.' Castaneda says, 'Are you sure I'm ready for it?' Don Juan says, 'You are because I give it to you.' Castaneda asks, 'What was it like for you?' 'It was the best I ever had, gave me power. I could fly. I was in the trees all day, and the Indians came from everywhere to watch me.' And Castaneda says, 'If it was that good for you why aren't you still on it?' Don Juan answers, 'What do you want me to do, spend all my life entertaining Indians?'"

This was an interesting incident to choose from the book, Charles, but your recollection of it was not quite correct. You significantly changed the meaning of what Castaneda has Don Juan finally say—a slip that says something about your own attitude on the subject. What Don Juan says is that he didn't want to spend all his life "frightening" Indians.

There are trees and then there are trees.

———

One afternoon we were sitting at my kitchen table when Paul Kugler came in. He was interested in starting a new literary magazine, he said, centering around your work. He asked you what you thought of the idea.

You were very enthusiastic. It fitted in perfectly with your often stated view that something new was happening now that you were teaching again. You reminded us that when you were at Black Mountain College there was *The Black Mountain Review,* and when you were at Buffalo there was *The Niagara Frontier Review.*

We spent an hour trying to think of an appropriate name for the new magazine. Most of the names we suggested were "dead," you said. You pointed out that there was "a guy in Chicago who does a magazine called *The Mojo Navigator.*" I asked you what the title meant.

"How the hell do I know what it means," you said, "but you've got to top it."

Finally you came up with what we all agreed was the perfect title, all things considered.

"Let's call it *The Dry Heaves,*" you said.

While we loved the title, we never did an issue.

"Who wants to write poetry all his life? I mean, you've got to be crazy to spend your whole life writing poetry."

Some nights you came out to my house instead of having dinner at the Altnaveigh. Once I invited you for dinner after your class. I was expecting you, therefore, at eleven—a midnight supper more or less. But you showed up at seven, looking a little desperate, and saying that you wanted "a drink, some soup, and some ideas," in that order.

I made some coffee for you, and put in the usual two teaspoons of sugar.

"You always remember exactly how I like it. How do you do it?" you asked.

I told you it was a pleasure to know your habits, and that it was important too, because someday people would want to know *everything* about Charles Olson.

"They will?" you laughed, with your usual false innocence.

Then came Thanksgiving, the only holiday in America that you liked. I had invited you to have dinner with us at my house. John and Glenis Lobb and their two small children were also to be guests. But you said you were going back to Gloucester that weekend and couldn't come.

When Germaine arrived for work at the Altnaveigh on Thanksgiving morning, however, she found you still there, looking downcast and complaining about lack of sleep. She scolded you for not going to visit someone for the holiday. She said the Inn would be packed all day with noisy customers and was no place for you. When you mentioned that you had been invited to my house, she urged you to call me up right away and go. You did.

It was about noon when the telephone rang.

"What size bore are you?" you asked before saying hello. You meant by this no slur, it turned out, but what size was my rifle this Thanksgiving morning, when you were going to play Indian, you said, and come storm my house and hill (Knowlton Hill). Would I accept an Indian for Thanksgiving dinner? You had been reading all about the history of this part of Connecticut, and were pretending now that I was Colonel Knowlton of Revolutionary War days, the man who had sent Nathan Hale, one of "Knowlton's Rangers," to spy on the British for General Washington.

I told you, Charles, that of course you were most welcome, that we needed your Indian very much, and reminded you that you had been invited in the first place. Colonel Knowlton, furthermore, had never shot an Indian in his life.

Moments later, you were at the door, and made a memorable day for all of us with your stories and talk. You sat by the fireplace in the same chair for the entire afternoon, wrapped in blankets because you were chilled, playing nonetheless with the children, drinking your favorite sherry (Duff Gordon No. 28) and a bottle of John Jameson Irish whiskey that you brought along for the occasion. You didn't eat much at dinner, only some dark meat from the turkey.

You complained about a soreness in your ear that was keeping you awake at night, which was why you had not returned to Gloucester.

Glenis Lobb was a physical therapist, and she finally convinced you that this was serious business and that you should see a doctor. You resisted the idea of doctors at first, but said you would make an appointment.

After the dishes were cleared away, we sat by the fire with brandy and cigars, the children sitting at your feet in inevitable awe.

The conversation that night was about Alfred North Whitehead. Lobb asked you if you had ever met him. You said you had. It was at a party in Boston, when you were a student at Harvard. You went up, you said, and tried to speak to him about his work, but the man was "too formal to let anybody talk to him about his work at a party."

I remembered how you never taught a course, or lectured very long, without insisting that everyone read Whitehead's *Process and Reality*. You would even tell students not to read the paperback edition of the book but to hunt around for old hardbound editions because this was a book you *had* to have hardbound, and "don't read the book until you have it!"

97

Even later on, in the hospital, scribbled feebly over and over again in your notes, your thoughts centered in Whitehead:

> The spiritual is all in Whitehead's simplest of all
> statements: Measurement is most possible
> throughout the system. That is what I mean.
> That is what I feel all inside. That is what is love.

If Carl Sauer was your geographer, Alfred North Whitehead was your philosopher. The Wesleyan University undergraduate curriculum in your day had been revamped along "general education" lines and Whitehead's book, published in your freshman year at Wesleyan, became one of the core texts in this curriculum. Its "philosophy of organism," its "subjectivist principle," and especially its scientifically minded efforts to offer a cosmology for the twentieth century, were facets of Whitehead's thinking that remained with you throughout your life.

After Whitehead, we asked you about Bertrand Russell. You said you had never met him, but never wanted to anyway. Russell was "a paltry man," you said. "I couldn't stand him."

Lobb then asked me if I had ever read Gaston Bachelard's *The Poetics of Space*. You practically jumped out of your seat.

"That's my title!" you said. How fascinated you were to hear that someone had written a phenomenological book on poetics.

Then the conversation drifted to your interest in the Atlantis myth again. Lobb asked you if you thought Plato really was remembering a historical place, or whether he was just telling stories. Was Mavor right?

"We'll never know what Plato was talking about," you said, with a finality that buried that topic forever.

It was an evening for book titles. Had you ever read Velikovsky's book on Akhnaten and Oedipus?

"Yeah," you said disparagingly, "science fiction."

At about nine o'clock, just as it was announced that the children had to go to bed, you unwrapped the blanket you sat huddled in and rose to leave. You gave everyone a great bear hug goodbye, and the one holiday you always kept was over.

On the day after Thanksgiving, the Lobbs and I went to the Altnaveigh for lunch. You came down (even at high noon this was a bit earlier than usual) and joined us. After lunch we sat at the table and talked away the remainder of the afternoon.

It was clear by now that you had taken complete charge of the place. The waitresses catered to every wish and special food that you requested. The owners, solicitous for your health and welfare, sat around listening to you for hours. Everyone was on an intimate first-name basis. I noticed with surprise that they were making bacon and eggs for you, a breakfast not on the menu—in fact the Altnaveigh never served breakfast to anybody. But for Charles Olson—anything!

You talked that afternoon mostly about England, especially the area around Dorset and Devon, which you had visited two years before. What you liked about the Altnaveigh and my own house, you said, was how their exposure on the land was so like the seaward exposure in Devon. You talked a lot about the lay of the land in Thomas Hardy's England, which so much of this part of Connecticut reminded you of, especially the way the hills continually shifted. You even recited for us Hardy's poem, "Going and Staying":

> . . . Seasons of blankness as of snow,
> The silent bleed of a world decaying,
> The moan of multitudes in woe,
> These were the things we wished would go;
> But they were staying . . .

The land absorbed you that day. You had been reading an article in a recent issue of *Scientific American*, which said that the earth had a protective covering over it that was like the skin of a man, and that this covering provided it with a resilience to meteorites and other disturbances. For some reason, however, the earth had started losing this skin, and in the not so distant future its resilience would be exhausted and the earth destroyed.

Mansfield, the town in which Storrs and several other little villages surrounding the University of Connecticut are officially incorporated, impressed you. You had studied its history in several books and tracked its geography on various maps. You preferred to call the town "Man's field."

"Don't you know you're living in Man's field?" you asked us.

You compared it to Devon. But then you wrote on the napkin, "Anywhere is everywhere."

You told us how you had recently visited the animal husbandry barns at the university, and how fascinated you were watching the staff there polling a "perfect" red calf. I think you liked the agricultural aspect of the University of Connecticut more than anything else. You were certainly not impressed by the place as any kind of intellectual center; on the other hand, given your contempt for the academic personality, I don't think any university today would have been to your liking in that respect. "Anywhere is everywhere" indeed.

You kept exploring the area, and you particularly admired the stone walls so often encountered along Connecticut roads. You would stop and try to date them, first by your own knowledge of the type of stones used and the way they were laid, then by asking the owners for the precise date. On more than one occasion you disagreed with the owner himself on the official date.

You told us that you had been writing a poem about all these things, and kept making little notes on the napkin. This is the poem:

> I live underneath
> the light of day
> I am a stone,
> or the ground beneath

My life is buried,
with all sorts of passages
both on the sides and in the face turned down to the earth
or built out as long gifted generous northeastern
    Connecticut stone walls are
through which 18th century roads still pass
as though they themselves were realms,
the stones they're made up of
are from the bottom such ice-age megaliths
and the uplands the walls on the boundaries of
are defined with such non-niggardly definition
of the amount of distance between, a road in & out
of the wood-lots or further passage-ways, further farms
are given

      that one suddenly is walking
in Tartarian-Erojan, Geaan-Ouranian
time and life   love space
   time & exact
analogy time & intellect   time & mind   time & time
          spirit
           the initiation
        of another kind of nation

    You kept saying that day that the important thing now was to be "well-tuned" to everything. It was especially important, you said, that poets be "well-tuned," in contrast to the generally passive way in which most people now lived their lives. You were proud of the breadth of your own incessant reading, and once even hectored an audience of your fellow poets in a lecture at Berkeley with the remark that their chief trouble was that they didn't read enough! It was a fair comment, coming from you, for you were plunderous with books, journals, newspapers, letters—anything with any information at all printed on it, anything that you could use.

    But you meant "well-tuned" in a certain physical sense as well, I think. The remark had sprung from the problem that the pain in your ear was giving you in sleeping and eating properly. You were quick to comment, too, on the irony that you were always telling people with problems and questions to "play it by ear."

This in turn had reminded me of a remark that the jockey, Will Hartack, had made earlier that year, when he was about to ride Majestic Prince in the Kentucky Derby. The television announcer had been interviewing all the jockeys before the race and had asked each one what strategy he intended to use in his ride that day. All the jockeys had elaborate schemes. But when Hartack was asked, he replied, simply, "I'll ride it by ear." He did, and of course won the race. When I told you this, you were delighted.

"Did he? Did he?" Then you said you remembered the race too, how Arts and Letters, the favorite, faded in the stretch, and how Dike and Majestic Prince came on. You laughed at the names. You had been talking before of Keats' remark that life was an allegory, how you believed it too, but not quite as Keats had meant it. This race was an allegory too. The whole country could be changed in a day, you said, if we could only name buildings the way we name race horses: The Dike Building, The Arts and Letters, The Majestic Prince.

Because we were on the subject of ears, and poets, you were reminded of a curious remark that Pound had made about Williams. "For a thing to go in one ear and out the other for Williams," Pound had said, "it has to go through his head," implying that Williams was slow. You laughed uproariously as you told us this little anecdote.

You described how Apple Records, the Beatles' company, had come to your apartment in Gloucester the previous spring for five days to make a tape of you reading your poems. You were impressed at the acoustical experience of reading with headphones on.

"There ought to be a law," you said, "that you only have to hear the sounds you make yourself. No other noise should be heard."

You put your hands over your ears and kept talking, telling us to do the same. "That's how we should hear ourselves."

The next day, you telephoned to ask me if I could use my influence to get a doctor to come out to the Altnaveigh to see you. I explained that unfortunately I had no influence with doctors, and that I doubted very much that any doctor would make a house call, especially when the complaint was only a pain in your ear.

"They'll come if *you* call them," you said.

As I suspected, the doctor I called wouldn't come out, so I made an appointment for you and you went in.

You told us later what a terrible experience it was for you to sit in the waiting room of the doctor's office surrounded by mothers and kids, having to wait your turn like everybody else. "It just goes to show you what a terrible state the world has come to," you said. "There are no priorities anymore."

The doctor decided that you needed an extensive series of tests that he thought would take about a week, and arranged for your admission to the Manchester Hospital, near Hartford.

It was now December 1st. You were admitted to Room 112 of the Manchester Hospital as patient number 293-479. You gave your weight as 255, but you actually weighed only 247. You told the nurse you had a severe pain over the left side of your face. They gave you a tablet of Percodan, which brought only slight relief. The initial diagnosis was trigeminal neuritis. After a more extensive examination, the doctor noted a trigger point of pressure over the exit of the mental nerve on the left chin reproducing the pain. You were then given large doses of Demerol, which still failed to relieve the pain. Your first night was very uncomfortable, sleeping only in naps, and taking Percodan frequently during the night.

When morning came, you felt even worse. You had headache and neuritis pains, and remained in bed.

I went in to see you the next day, and each day thereafter, bringing mail and the news, and asking for whatever report they may have given you on how you were. No one at that time had any idea of the seriousness of your illness, and you were unfailingly merry whenever I went in. At most we thought you had an ear infection.

You shared your room in the Manchester Hospital with a very pleasant Italian shoemaker, who had emigrated to this country from Florence when he was in his twenties. You were delighted with him because he told so many stories about Italy and his life there. As always, you took great pleasure in people with stories to tell.

"Storytellers are the only people who have experienced anything in life," you once declared.

But the shoemaker was to be a patient only a few days and soon left. Afterwards, you spoke fondly of him, but pointed out that while he told many stories of his youth in Italy, he never told anything about his life in this country. His whole life, you said, was in his youth, before America. America had made absolutely no impression on him—or at least none that was worth talking about.

"He should never have left Italy," you said

You next shared the room with a man we'll call McCormack, a plant manager at a firearms company. Whenever I would go into the room, this man would have his entire family visiting: his son from Vietnam, in a much-decorated uniform, his wife in her fur coat, and each day a new assortment of other relatives. They never said much to each other. They usually just sat there, on their side of the room in silence. It was obvious as well that they didn't like the boisterous giant who was in bed next to them; nor, need it be said, did the giant like them.

As soon as I would arrive, however, and you exclaimed some hearty greeting ("How the hell are ya?"), we would start talking our "business," as oblivious of their sour stares as we could be under the circumstances.

You were very interested at the time in Egyptian etymologies, and we talked about the word for Egypt itself, which you said meant "The Soul of the House of Ptah." We carried on through the whole two hours one night—noisily, excitedly, crazily—talking about this etymology.

The McCormack family just sat there, sometimes mumbling to each other, most of the time glaring at us. This went on for several days. Then one night I arrived to find that you had your room all to yourself. I asked what had happened to your roommate. You said that the hospital had suddenly decided to make this into a private room, which is what you wanted in the first place. I was surprised, because we had tried diligently to get you a private room originally and the hospital refused. Then you explained what had happened.

McCormack, it turned out, was suffering from an inflamed testicle. And he thought you were suffering from a brain tumor! Every night, after I would leave, and you got up to go to the bathroom, you would leave the door open a crack. You could hear McCormack telling the nurse that you were crazy, that the two of us in fact were crazy! Finally, you said, you had enough. You leaned over the bed that night, pulled back the curtain between the beds, and said, "Listen, McCormack, if you don't shut up and stop telling the nurse that I'm crazy, I'm going to get up out of this bed and come over there and squeeze you know what!"

McCormack was scared, and didn't say anything, but the next night when you got up to go to the bathroom, you left the door open a crack again and could hear McCormack telling the nurse something. After she left, you walked over to his bed, pulled back the curtain again, and said, "Okay, McCormack, you know what I told you!"

At this point the man started screaming for help and they had to take him out and give him another room. You finally had a room to yourself.

You were given an endless battery of tests. X-rays were taken of the chest, ribs, and jaw, with no remarkable findings. An electrocardiogram was normal. A kidney test was done and the kidneys were found normal. But when you came back from these tests you were perspiring. You became uncooperative with the nurses who were trying to prepare you for further X-ray treatment, and you refused to abide by the rule against eating. As if by some magic power of your will, however, a tray of food was delivered by mistake. When the nurse noticed it, and demanded it be taken away, you refused. You weren't going to let Big Nurse bully you out of your supper! Only after the doctor came in, with special pleading, would you allow the tray to be taken away.

Just after you entered the hospital that first week, you asked me to take over your seminar. It was only to be for that week since you expected to be back on the job shortly. I suggested that you simply skip it for a week, which you were certainly entitled to do because of your illness, but you were worried about its continuity. You were particularly concerned that the English Department not think you were abandoning them.

I agreed to take over the class and asked what you wanted me to talk about.

"Just tell them about me," you said. "Tell them who I am."

The class was disappointed that night when I walked in without you. There were about a dozen people in all, one or two who had come apparently as visitors, and who had never seen you.

We talked mostly about the emphasis on local history in your poetry. Some students said that they felt turned off by "the Gloucester" in Olson, by what they thought of as an excessive attention to local matters. If you're not from Gloucester, was the implication, it's hard to get excited about it all.

This view, of course, was shared by others beyond this classroom, and you surely must have heard it all before, for if your poems were praised to the skies in some little magazines of the Fifties and Sixties, they rarely fared so well in the infrequent reviews of major journals, where you were treated superficially, if at all.

You were a lyric poet, and a commanding one, though even your early poems failed to impress the conventional reader of the fifties who came to your work looking for the usual symbols, and coded meanings, the gnarled rhetoric that was characteristic of the poetry of those years. Oh, the paraphernalia of the New Criticism—how you hated it! The so-called Black Mountain School had been lumped together with the rest of the outsiders of the Fifties, especially the Beats, as the "unwashed" versus the "washed," or the "raw" versus the "cooked," or the "Establishment" versus the "anti-Establishment." There were many such polarities set up at the time, rather naively it would seem now, to discriminate against those poems that didn't score sufficiently high on somebody's niceness machine.

Though your poetry was for the most part free of these academic games, it presented difficulties of another kind. Your whole sense of poetry was gradually moving from lyric to "epic"—a term that applies to Pound's *Cantos* and Williams' *Paterson* as well. Modern "epic" poetry had become a world all its own, and one that few critics, at least at first, have had the patience, capacity, or interest to endure. Facing the lyric bias of modern poetry, and of modern poetry criticism, *The Maximus Poems* have often been met with the same dismay that greeted these earlier works. Yet the "epic" scope of your poems, like Pound's and Williams', is extraordinarily individualized and rests in the end on the same highly Romantic assumptions about the nature of a poem and the man making it as does the simpler form of the lyric.

You outlined your own jumping off point in a critique of the *Cantos* and *Paterson* in your *Mayan Letters:*

Ez's epic solves problem by his ego: his single emotion breaks all down to his equals or inferiors (so far as I can see only two, possibly, are admitted, by him, to be his betters—Confucius, and Dante. Which assumption, that there are intelligent men whom he can outtalk, is beautiful because it destroys historical time, and thus creates the methodology of the Cantos, viz, a space-field where, by inversion, though the material is all time material, he has driven through it so sharply by the beak of his ego, that, he has turned time into what we must now have, space and its live air

the primary contrast, for our purpose is, BILL: his Pat is exact opposite of Ez's, that is, Bill HAS an emotional system which is capable of extensions and comprehensions the ego-system (the Old Deal, Ez as Cento Man, here dates) is not. Yet by making his substance historical of one city (the Joyce deal), Bill completely licks himself, lets time roll him under as Ez does not, and thus, so far as what is the more important, methodology, contributes nothing, in fact, delays, deters, and hampers, by not having busted through the very problem which Ez has so brilliantly faced, and beat

What you mean by "methodology" here, I told your class, has much to do with what you mean by "history." Your view of history, which *The Maximus Poems* embody, is best elucidated in your book, *Special View of History,* based on several lectures you gave at Black Mountain in the 1950s, and published posthumously. They inform us considerably of the Romantic cast of your thinking.

You argue in these lectures that "like it or not, see it or not, history is the *function* of any one of us." Each individual life has an historical function; the value of that life is rendered intense as history, and only as history (no less existentialist a position is conceivable). And properly, you pay homage, in this Romantic view, to Keats:

The other epigraph is a methodological one. Keats, more than Goethe or Melville, faced with the Man of Power, got to the heart of it. He took the old humanism by the right front. It wasn't the demonism of Genius he saw was the hooker (almost nobody yet has caught up with Keats on the same subject—he was almost the only man who has yet seen the subjective tragedy as no longer so interesting), but the very opposite, the Sublime in the Egotistical, the very character of Genius, its productive power. And as he walked home from the mummer's play Christmas 1818 it struck him he believed in nothing else, I mean Negative Capability. When a man is "capable of being in uncertainties, mysteries, doubts, without any irritable reaching after fact and reason . . ."

With Keats, you saw the value of the mythological, of "muthos," over that "irritable reaching after fact and reason" to which, you thought, fifth-century Greek philosophers and seventeenth-century physicists had yoked us. The mythological had been displaced by the rational, with consequent loss in the intensity of any of us.

Thus, history being our proper function, and "muthos" being what you called "the kosmos inside a human being," the special view of history is special indeed: it is mythology. We are all, "like it or not, see it or not," myth-making. And where we come together, in our myth-making, is "the new localism," which is to say, for Charles Olson, Gloucester, Massachusetts:

History is the new localism, a polis to replace the one which was lost in various stages all over the world from 490 B.C. on, until anyone of us knows places where it is disappearing right now. Man is estranged from that with which he is most familiar, the man said, and it must have been apparent to Heraclitus that a part of it at least was the beginning of the loosening of the old place, he bit Miletus's behind so savagely when he also said of his own people, They are too filthy as citizens to pay attention.

In the story you wrote about your father's life as a postman, and never published, you refer affectionately to the sense of history which your father first gave you:

It was the Mathew Bradys my father gave me as a child that have influenced my sense of the past to this day. I have the set. It was the *Review of Reviews* issue of the Photographic History. They came, by subscription, I suppose, as thin, large, blue paperbound pamphlets which I could lay open page by page on the floor. The photographs cured me that early of romantic history. I preferred Brady to the colored frontispiece each one carried of some fool's oil on Grant at Lookout Mt or Burnside at Nashville.

And you point out in this story, which was written before you had begun the *Maximus* series of poems, how your father's own sense of American history finally "localized" on Gloucester:

I wonder now what Brady did for him. Maybe, just because I was born here, I had the jump on him. He valued America, as immigrants do, more than the native. I'm not sure it's a good thing. It wasn't in my father's case, as this trouble he got himself into will show, though for me his fascination with the story of this country was fruitful, as it sometimes is, in the second generation American. There is a sentimentality about the freedoms of this country which none of the bitterness of poverty and abuse will shake in an immigrant. My father had it, at least up to this trouble I write about when the government of these States so failed him he was thrown back on that other rock of the immigrant, his foreign nationality organizations. It took something out of my father's historical soul. [The word "romantic" was crossed out here and "historical" substituted.—C.B.] From then on he localized his interest to the past of Gloucester and the fishing industry. That, I think, was a gain and, had he lived, it would have given his life and his painting a ground. That was a more usable, economic America than the society of the rights of man which failed him.

Whatever the Mathew Brady photographs did for your father, something of the romantic having been taken out of his soul, they seem to have had a different effect, ultimately, on you. For though the pages of *The Maximus Poems* are flush with the facts and dates of Gloucester history, you are no photographic realist at heart. Yours is the most personal (you would probably say "personalized") view of history imaginable. It is finally a lyric view of history, a lyric view of "polis," and Gloucester is Charles Olson's polis, where he acts, or makes his story.

Your sense of *The Maximus Poems* as "epic" has to be seen in this "personalized" light. With epic, in at least the ancient sense, a poet transcends merely private interests, private experiences, private visions. The epic poet need not rely on the authority of his own identity for an order to what he is saying. Yet your view of myth and history, though aiming at a public mode, only took you away, in the end, from such a transcendence of private matters. It could not have been otherwise. In many respects, and not surprisingly, no one could be more uniquely private than the author of *The Maximus Poems*. For you, the polis of Gloucester, and its history, had become the nearest field of coherence to your own self. A strictly lyric poet, of course, would have stopped with his own self. The advantage, of course, in not stopping there is the considerable gain in range (you would say in "intensity") that is the hallmark of the modern epic poet.

The Maximus Poems are, after all, an attempt to usurp the loneliness and despair, the aimlessness, the rootlessness, that is "the subjective tragedy," a theme that runs on lamentably throughout the poetry of this century. They are exploratory, of course, and they are didactic; but beyond all else they are celebrations—every

---

III

line is a celebration of this man in his history, in his city, in his self. But they are, alas, celebrations for an elite:

> Polis now
> is a few, is a coherence not even yet new (the island
> of this city is a mainland now of who? who can say who are
> citizens?

The poems as a series have no simple beginning or end (*The Cantos* and *Paterson* at least begin clearly enough). Their order must ultimately go back to the will of the man setting them, to where he happens to be. They are epic by accumulated effect, lyric by design. One has the sense of mass, but the order is a personal one. We are not reading "the Gloucester" in Olson so much as "the Olson" in Gloucester.

The class at any rate lasted about two hours, and then I drove back to the hospital, as you had asked me to, to tell you about it. You were beaming, sitting at the edge of the bed waiting for me when I walked in.

"What did you say? What did you tell them about me? How did it go?"

As I told you some of the things I had said, you became quite amused, whether with pleasure or scorn I'll never know. You interrupted several times with "And?"—meaning, "and what did the students say to that?"

In spite of a prolific output, you never won any of the prizes awarded each year to poets and writers, though in the last decade of your life your work became, without question, more influential with younger writers than that of any other American poet. When the second volume of *The Maximus Poems* came out in 1968, I told you that this book, surely, would obtain for you some of the honors you deserved.

"Nah, don't count on it," you said. "But I'll tell you a little story. There was once a man who came home drunk one night so late that he saw only the milkman and his horse making the early morning deliveries. As the man was fumbling with his keys on the porch, he heard the horse suddenly address him, saying, 'What are you doing there, stupid?' The man turned around and, delighted, started talking to the horse. While they were talking, the man suddenly realized how astonishing it was that this horse was actually talking. A talking horse! 'Hey, you're fantastic!' the man said, 'an actual talking horse!' To which the horse replied: 'That ain't nothin'—I also won the Kentucky Derby!' "

Your students at the University started coming out to the hospital now, and friends came from out of state as well. The room was fast filling up with them. To us, you seemed to be enjoying it all—the attention, the comfort of being forced to stay in bed all day, the personalities on the hospital staff whose lives you lost no time in exploring.

You were holding royal court, propped up in bed on a half-dozen pillows like an Oriental potentate greeting each one as if he had crossed the steppes of Asia to see you with news of his own distant kingdom. Hospitals were times of assessment for you. You had occupied several of them at key points in your life and they furnished, if nothing else, a pleasant opportunity to gather your clan anew. Some of your friends, you said, only seemed to see you in hospitals. You would quickly make everyone feel at home, offer them the food off your tray, serve them juices or ginger ale from the whole wagonload of beverages you insisted the nurses leave with you for your giant thirst. Like Gulliver in Lilliput, you found that a normal-sized paper cup offered only a drop of refreshment.

"Isn't it grand," you said at one point, "just like the good old days in Millard Fillmore."

You were referring to a month-long hospitalization in Buffalo when your following came nightly and in droves to see you, to the utter consternation of the hospital staff. And in particular you recalled the night in Millard Fillmore Hospital when Charles Brover and I talked to you in your room until visiting hours were over, and you suddenly decided to walk us downstairs to the lobby. We sat in the lobby talking until midnight, at which point you were going to put on your overcoat (it was mid-winter) and come out and have a drink with us. It was a crazy idea—you were ill with emphysema at the time—but you were serious.

"The nurses think I'm sound asleep upstairs, they'll never miss me, come on, let's go." You had more to say, more to talk about. We finally convinced you to go back to bed.

I tried frequently to find out from you, in Manchester, what was wrong, what were the doctors telling you, where was your pain coming from. Most of the time you would reply, "It's only me. It's nothing. It's only me."

It was a strange thing to say. I didn't think that it was someone else who was suffering. How sharply you seemed to distinguish your body as something separate from yourself.

"The body is inside the soul," you said, a line of Pound's you quoted over and over. And now it was as if you thought of yourself as some kind of externalized soul—or internalized body? I thought at the time of your "Human Universe" essay, where you write so eloquently of feeling and how the Mexicans of Yucatan would jostle you and each other on the bus with an ease of common feeling all but unknown to the rest of us anymore. "The admission these people give me and one another," you wrote, "is direct, and the individual who peers out from that flesh is precisely himself, is a curious wandering animal like me—it is so very beautiful how animal human eyes are when the flesh is not worn so close it chokes, how human and individuated the look comes out of a human eye when the house of it is not exaggerated."

John Cech, one of your graduate students, visited one night at the hospital wearing heavy workboots, and upon entering your room accidentally stepped on your bare feet which were dangling halfway across the floor. You didn't even wince. Cech apologized instantly, and more than once, until you said, "Oh don't worry about *that*, that's just the tip of the iceberg."

Lee Kugler came to see you again, and you had a long talk. Among other things, you told her, "Ride your depressions right down to the bottom, baby—when you get there they don't exist."

You received a present, in the Manchester Hospital, of a book called *The Key*, by John Cohane, which had just come out. This book, through a rather interesting series of etymological maneuvers, argues a great primeval diaspora in which the same basic language was carried to all corners of the world, where traces of it can still be found. Cohane interconnects Avon, Stonehenge, Mycenae, Barbados, Borneo, and even Mystery Hill in New Hampshire, to mention but a few, as places of possible ancient wandering by this people.

It was just the sort of book you loved. You said that Cohane bore out what you were yourself thinking about for some time— the migration of various Semitic tribes as far as Polynesia. *The Key* was a book that fit perfectly the Laurentian perspective in your imagination. It made you talk about the Pacific, which you disliked. You said you never wanted to go there, that it was unfriendly—unlike the Atlantic—and the source of earthquakes.

The Pacific, you said, was the womb, and primitive, and the moon came out of it. You were a man for Atlantic waters only.

In the margins of *The Key*, you started to keep track of each day's events now, your feelings, your thoughts. Here is one of the first entries:

> Friday Dec. 5 LXIX Hospital Connecticut
> Constant and careful now and forever (There) after
>
> To be to extricate the (soul) from all
> other   problems of appetite?
>   desires
>   sleep etc.
> To keep the mixtures (sansara?   self conception
> and instead let it have its life by making sure
> (what solitude very obviously does
> —as company equally makes one healthy
>   —work for me now
>
>
>   or
>   Time spent simply for itself wastes one in
>   one's own souls
>
>   nature &
>   special needs   poetry- = now
>   Mythology
>
> Actually place things out in front of me
> They should be placed there in front of one's
> self (as in Pleistocene

Another entry may have been made in reference to your former hospital roommate, McCormack, whom you clearly didn't like:

Sunday
Those hard-eyed late Yankees
who are not sure of themselves
at all. But, as a late elite,
have to exhibit animus in the face
of new American force

       the sweet inner way of life (as of who 'feels'
      about what I do as I do)—or participates
    in them as though from the same inside
         (Sun-Mon
         Dec. 6th - 7th
         -LXIX

Mon. a.m.
     They are simply dehumanized
and selfish ignorant artificial creations
    not even an
Pietudes—and practices

One of the tests in the Manchester Hospital involved your lying under a machine that prints out a total physical description of the patient in eight minutes. You told me how excited you were by this, and commented on its possibilities for a writer.

"Think of it," you said, "in eight minutes it gives you this flat clean prose—the best prose being written today—telling you all about yourself. For years I've been trying to do this kind of thing and look, it takes them only eight minutes on anybody. Can you beat that!"

You kept the print-out in a table drawer near your bed, and took it out to show anyone who came in asking how you were.

That night you made the following entry about the print-out in the margins of *The Key:*

           My levy
    like saying the inside of me
       printed direct

My soul really exists—it is me when physically
I am spectographic and intellectually my words
saving me   descry   intelligend
one
Mon. Dec. 8th

You became increasingly interested now in working out a statement on myth, and began making extensive notes on the subject,
incorporating into them your dreams at this time, along with
those of others. And in particular you remembered that walk we
took in the woods behind my house at Knowlton Hill, and the
mythological overtones it had for you:

Tues night December 9th
1969

conditio

The analytical   analogy
(time and exact definition
consequential nature of
and the abstract
form in the
expression
(impetus
each going moment
initiatic cosmos,   world of nature,   celestial world
(cosmology)   (theology)

nature
poetry as acts
(conditions of personal being)
mythology (conditions of image and narrative,
(of some gods?):
and of public-private
action
(condition of)
dreams'   instructional statements

118

archetypal dreams: example, of Rome last
week (Charles Boer's dream
of "And the cicadas mate
in the air"
(language of the Unconscious

      poetry   \

              ⌐ myth

? ⎯⎯⎯⎯⎯⎯⎯⎯⎯⎯⎯⎯⎯⎯⎯

The moment you've made that selection
You've called attention to it and so ruined
the beauty or other reason of choosing it

Mythological powers as such
  (performs form
or narrative or image forms in
the real, in either the process of their creations:
         trees
         men (ex. Melville - and Homer? Also who
         dreams
         paintings
         buildings or sculptures: ex. Parthenon
         layunders: Rome below earth's level
                  as well as some street distances
         Mts. river streams pools sacred groves
             oak (Dodona,
             Knowlton Hill,
             Connecticut

    The doctors decided to perform a liver biopsy. It was earlier
noticed that your liver was larger than usual, but this was at first
attributed to the fact that you were such a big man. You tolerated
the painful biopsy procedure very well, and when it was over, you
said to the doctor, grandly, "You are the only man that has ever
penetrated the inner sanctum of my liver!"
    It took a couple of days to get the results, and by this time it
was becoming a matter of routine for me to ask you what the findings were that day, only to have you say, "They don't know yet."

When I went in to ask you if the biopsy results were in yet, you said, rather nonchalantly, "Yeah."

"Well, what's the word?" I asked.

"It's curtains," you said suddenly, but so easily, as if this meant only the end of some game, or some petty robbery at which you finally got caught; as if the phrase itself didn't mean death.

I was shocked and went blank for a minute. The ease with which you said it made me think for a second that maybe it meant something else. I sat down, just looking at you, not knowing at all what to say. Finally I asked what "It's curtains" meant. What was wrong?

"Cancer of the liver," you shot back, as calmly as before. I didn't move. I didn't cry out at these totally unexpected and devastating words, because you suddenly added, "Now here's what I want you to do," and started telling me in great detail about your children, your poems, your papers; what to do with the car; everything that must be considered by a man who suddenly has to straighten things out. It took an hour, maybe two hours, sitting there, listening to you wrap up your life in front of me—or unwrap it—for this final complete look. And how easily you seemed to do it! How easily you got me to participate in this sad conversation with you, as if it were only a matter of routine business. I can never forget it.

It was inconceivable that now, at 59, you were about to die. I was stunned. I refused to believe it, although it was clear that you believed it. There was, you said, nothing that could really be done for you, though everything would be tried. The official medical report read: "Hepatoma-Grade 1"—a primary cancer of the liver.

I was astonished, always, at the coolness, the ease of the man, Charles Olson, whenever I talked to you on subsequent days, or when other visitors talked to you. Yet you were not so easy or so cool with your doctors. That first night, after the fatal report was announced, you had no complaints, and slept comfortably throughout the night. The next morning, however, the doctors found you very upset, and crying out at them angrily.

You asked me to return the Plymouth Fury to the Avis Company, and gave me the key to drive it back from the hospital lot where you had left it. The bill was obviously going to be in the hundreds of dollars (it was, in fact, $880). You wanted me to find out if a deal could be arranged whereby they would apply your payment for the rental to an outright purchase from them of the car. They had sent you several notices by this time, each one more threatening than before, warning you to return the car or face arrest.

"Tell them I got plague and they'll probably give it to me!" you said.

That you wanted to buy the car from them seemed strange considering that you knew now the hopelessness of your condition. But I didn't question the point with you and set off to find the car.

It was nine o'clock at night and extremely cold out when I left the hospital to look for it. It was always a rude jolt to come out of that deliberately overheated hospital into the fresh but freezing air of the street. Snow had begun to fall, the first of a long and gloomy winter. The snow made it hard to differentiate the cars in the parking lot.

I combed all the hospital lots that night, and even the side streets, but found no Plymouth Fury. When I got home I called the police in Manchester, to ask if they had towed it from the hospital, but they said that they had a policy of not towing cars from the hospital area. They added, however, that perhaps the hospital itself had towed it, as they sometimes do, and to check with them. I checked with them the next morning by phone, and they said they didn't know if they had towed it, that they didn't think they had towed it, but to check with the garage in Manchester where they take cars when they do tow them. I checked with the garage and they didn't have it.

Paul Kugler and I then drove to the hospital in the afternoon. We went up to ask you again for more specific directions as to where you had left it. You were being examined by one of the doctors, however, and we decided not to bother you.

We drove all over the hospital area again, looking for the car, but still couldn't find it. Finally we decided to talk to the manager of the hospital about it. I was wearing an old trench coat, and when I told the manager, in his office, that we were looking for a 1969 Plymouth Fury reportedly left on his lot, the first thing he said was, "You cops?"

"No, poets," I said, not being able to resist, and perhaps slipping into a protective sense of the absurd that this mounting contact with hospital bureaucracy was developing in me. The hospital manager was no help. Kugler suggested we call Avis and ask them if they had taken the car or at least to report it as stolen. I called them, and indeed they had taken it. I told them, as instructed, that you were in the hospital with plague. They said they were sorry to hear that, but no deals about buying it were possible.

Your notes in the margins of *The Key* now assumed a more final tone than before:

> history as time
>   alchemy of
> slain kings roots
>   planets
> "through time and exact definition"
>   (explicitness and
> analogy like to like
>
> the Lake Van Measure
>   I reject nothing. I accept it all (though
>   there on rejected. What man's senses of
>   examples—the demonstrative categories of

employment which have all descended into the
organization—of Time for plutocratic
purposes and the result is the Americans are
simply examples of the 7 Deadly sins) One
means rather smelling entirely different—
both a fantastic sweetened possible difference
development, inner powers and
explanations. The spiritual is all in Whitehead's
simplest of all statements: Measurement is
most possible throughout the system. That is
what I mean. That is what I feel all inside.
That is what is love.
                    Charles, Saturday morning
                    December 13th
                    LXIX

It was hard at first for some of your visitors to accept the fact that
you were so ill. Your exuberance at seeing them, from the moment
they got to the door, was boundless. In many ways, you seemed
more energetic than ever, and the fact that you would always dismiss your illness as insignificant made it even easier to forget that
this performance—one of your finest—was taking place in a hospital room. Few visitors were aware of the real nature of your suffering.

You had even redecorated the room, turning over a bland hos-
pitalesque painting on the wall so that the plain wooden backside,
daubed as it was with a few smears of bright paint, faced you. The
"painting" was more interesting this way, and people admired it.
The Olson touch.

But performance it all was. What we didn't know was that when
the last visitor would leave for the night, you would ring and even
scream for the nurses to bring morphine for the pain. The doctor
who took care of you at this time told me later that because you
were in such exceptional pain he authorized you to have up to
eight times the ordinary dose for someone in this condition. The

nurses used to question this, he said, not being able to believe he would authorize such large doses. He emphasized that this would start immediately after the last of us had left.

One evening Charles Brover went to see you, along with a colleague, Tom Churchill, who had written a hostile review of the movie "Easy Rider" for the *UCONN Free Press.* You were impressed with the review and wanted to meet him. The talk was again of radical politics, with many of the same arguments that had been exchanged earlier at Brover's house making the rounds once more. Neither of you would be budged from his earlier position. But when it was time to go, Brover walked over to the bed to shake hands with you. Both of you were conscious of the fact that it might be the last time you would see each other. Brover was wearing a button on the lapel of his coat that said "Smash Racism." You read the button, but said nothing to him for a minute. Then, squeezing his hand, and nodding to the button, you said, almost under your breath, "Good luck."

I once told you of an old Greek expression, "You always get the gods you deserve."

You replied, "You only get the gods that are."

Paul Kugler had added to this, "You always get the women you deserve."

You replied, "You only get the women that are."

The expression came up again in one of your final entries in *The Key:*

> Mon night Dec. 15th still Manchester
> How far down one has to go
> to get the gods which are
> —seed water (Eros) which creates (as thought-earth,

                    the Heavenly Heart
                    of the Middle Kingdom
                    <u>substantivizes</u>
fundamentum. The value. The root of the
Heavenly Tree—and that clear shining water
in those three Goddesses' hands: Morta
                                  Nona
                                  Decima
(and that the man of the Heavenly Tree
—Ymir—
is the true Hector and here,
simply one's body, man,
or gigantic iotunn
the size of man as the Tree the
size of Earth Demeter
both above and below—thought—
himself.

You were by now in great pain. The nurses noted on your record
that at times you seemed frightened. You required frequent shots.
It was finally suggested that a surgical operation on the liver might
be tried to save your life. Even without surgery, however, you
were assured several months to live. Or so the doctors thought.
The Manchester doctors recommended that the surgery be done
at New York Hospital, where the finest specialists in this kind of
operation reside.

At first you accepted the idea outright. Arrangements would be
made for a transfer to New York. A few days before the transfer
was to be made, however, you decided against it.

You were unable to eat, though the staff noted that you were
always cheerful with visitors. They found this encouraging. On
the 16th of December you were sleepless and smoked heavily
through the night. You were given medication frequently, and
kept asking for things to "stop my mind."

That day you talked at length with your doctor about your future as a writer.

"I need ten more years to finish my work," you told him.

You decided again to go ahead with the transfer to New York for the possibility of surgery. The next day, however, you were again very angry with the staff. The pain in your ear, and now in your liver, was unbearable. You slept only two hours that night. When you awoke on the 18th, very drowsy, your speech was somewhat slurred. You wanted a hypo and your yellow pain pills at the same time. This was the day of the big move to New York.

When it was finally decided that you would be moved to the New York Hospital, Harvey Brown offered to do it in his station wagon, which was large enough to put a mattress in if you felt like riding in front. You agreed to this, and Harvey drove down from Massachusetts with his station wagon.

Harvey was another friend from Buffalo days, and you were glad to see him. He had started a publishing company, Frontier Press, to promote the work of poets and writers.

The doctors felt that you didn't need an ambulance for the trip to New York, although surely, we thought, this would have been the most comfortable way for you to travel, and the ambulance drivers, we thought, would be prepared for emergencies that we were not. But it's always difficult, it seems, to arrange for ambulances at hospitals, and doctors don't seem to recommend them unless the patient is virtually unconscious. We debated the choice for awhile, and decided that we would order an ambulance after all, if only because the professionals would be better equipped for this sort of thing. As it turned out, we were utterly wrong.

There was also the problem of making sure that a room would be available in the New York Hospital upon arrival, and the two had to be synchronized. You told Harvey and me to go back to my house, and that you would call us the next day when the ambulance and room were ready, telling us to be ready to move the moment you called.

The next day, about noon, the telephone rang and I answered. The voice on the other end exclaimed heartily, "This is Olson-Action-Motion! Are you ready on your end?"

We rushed to the hospital to find you still packing things up in those extra-large paper sacks hospitals provide. Your son, Charles Peter, and your daughter, Kate, were there, along with an aunt. Charles Peter had been living in Gloucester with relatives since his mother died, and Kate was living in Philadelphia with her mother.

We sat around for awhile waiting for the ambulance to appear. You seemed very alert but calm. The doctors had all come in to talk to you and to say goodbye. Finally, the ambulance arrived and the drivers came in with a seven-foot stretcher. First, however, they asked for a check to cover the fare for the ride. You wrote the check and got on the stretcher. You had already given the nurses a $25 tip, which at first they refused, but which you insisted they take for a Christmas party. Most of the paper sacks were piled onto fifteen-year-old Charles Peter, who seemed happy to carry them. We all squeezed into the hospital elevator, the six of us standing around the stretcher looking down at you, completely wrapped in blankets, with only your face peering out, the paper sacks all piled around you on the stretcher. You smiled up at us. "What a sight," you said.

It was very cold out, and there was some unfortunately slow juggling at the ambulance door, since you insisted on riding forward, and going in feet first. ("Never get yourself in a position where you have to go backward," you once told me, in Gloucester, when I borrowed your old Chevy one night, only to find that it had no reverse on it.)

I sat next to you in the ambulance facing forward, and Harvey sat backward, facing you. Charles Peter and Kate, who would not be coming to New York for a few days yet, came up to the windows and waved goodbye. We were off.

You seemed to feel fine at first. You were looking forward to the move, or rather to the motion of the ride, having been in the Manchester Hospital for over two weeks. You had been given a pill just before, one of what you always referred to as your "yellow-jackets."

We drove past Hartford, the ambulance going at a normal speed, and down the Wilbur Cross Highway south to New York. After a half hour or so, you decided to sit up in order to look out the window and enjoy the view of the countryside. You talked cheerfully, smoked a little, and seemed very much your old self.

You talked of many things, speculated on how long it had been since you were in New York, and what a return this was. At one point you suggested that the driver play the ambulance siren, to announce to New York that "Olson's coming!" The driver said he wasn't allowed to do that sort of thing.

We drove past Middletown, which reminded you of your undergraduate days at Wesleyan, thirty-five years before. The subject switched to politics and you told us of a "dirty business" that was going on in New York with the U.S. district attorney there, Robert Morgenthau, whom you knew from some distant part of your political past. Morgenthau was a good man, you said, a man of real integrity, and "there aren't *any* of his kind left around any-more." John Mitchell, you said, Nixon's attorney general, was out to get Morgenthau, and in fact had got him, because Morgenthau was suddenly being replaced by a Mitchell appointee. Mitchell, who had a law practice in New York before Nixon acquired him, hated everything that Morgenthau stood for, you said. "Filthy business, filthy business." It was Olson the political observer talk-ing, and it sounded heartening that, with all you had to endure now, you could still keep up such mundane interests.

You were gulping down the ice water, and finished the whole pitcher before we were even half way. You would lie down again periodically and rest for awhile, then sit up abruptly and continue talking. After one such rest you suddenly sat up, looked out the window a moment, and then recited, with great drama, and to my absolute astonishment and pleasure, the following speech from *King Lear:*

Poor naked wretches, whereso'er you are,
That bide the pelting of this pitiless storm,
How shall your houseless heads and unfed sides,
Your looped and windowed raggedness, defend you
From seasons such as these? O, I have ta'en
Too little care of this! Take physic, pomp;
Expose thyself to feel what wretches feel,
That thou mayst shake the superflux to them
And show the heavens more just.

I could only marvel, Charles, at the greatness of your heart that
you should come up with *that* speech from *that* play on this cold-
est of winter days in an ambulance now drifting into the gloom of
New York where you must certainly have realized your life would
soon end. You lay down again on the stretcher and went to sleep.

About a half hour later you awoke and said you were in pain,
that the pill they had given you had worn off and you needed
another. But there were no others. The hospital wouldn't allow
any to be sent along, and there weren't even aspirins, the driver
now telling us that they weren't allowed to carry anything.

You were groaning from the pain. You lay there, holding tightly
to my hand, squeezing it white. You asked if we could radio ahead
to the hospital to have one of your "yellow-jackets" ready the moment we arrived. But the radio was not in touch with the hospital.

Every few minutes you asked, "Are we there yet?" We would try
to assure you that it would only be minutes now, though the ambulance was going slower and slower as it got nearer to the city,
and the driver was having problems with directions. This turned
out to be the first trip he had ever made to New York! Harvey
Brown, who had lived there, had to direct him.

You told us that the moment we arrived we were to go into the
hospital and get the doctors to send out a pill before you were
moved from the ambulance. And you made us promise that we
would do this, no matter what. We promised.

It was a long ride, and your agony seemed unendurable. You
kept squeezing my hand tighter and tighter as you felt the pain,

and we had to keep making false assurances that it would only take another few minutes. The traffic in the city now only stumbled along, and at some points moved not at all. It was awful.

Finally, in the dark of early evening, we arrived. The trip from Manchester had taken nearly four hours. We went in to ask for medicine, to *demand* medicine, but got no help from the staff, who sharply informed us that no patient was given any medicine until he was examined. No exceptions. We decided to get you to your room as soon as possible, ignoring as best we could your plea from the stretcher for "yellow-jackets."

It was dark in the hospital, which was enormous. Visitors were coming down in the elevators to go home. One of them had to tell our ambulance driver where to find the elevator for the twelfth floor, which was where we were to take you. It was in another corridor. We found it, waiting endlessly for it to come, wondering after a while if it were out of order.

You remained quiet, enduring the pain now in silence. They finally wheeled you into your room, a dimly lighted little cubicle that you shared with someone else, who wasn't there. The plaster was peeling from the walls in certain places, an old steam heater by the window overheating the room unbearably, and, inevitably, the bed was a foot too short! It was all a disappointment, and we knew it immediately. I remembered an old biker's expression, "You only roll as good as you look," and I knew that this place wasn't going to roll at all.

You told Harvey to give the ambulance drivers a twenty dollar tip, which he did, and they left, wishing you well. Harvey left too, to make a phone call.

A nurse came in, and you immediately insisted that you be given something for the pain, but she refused toughly, and said that it would have to wait for the doctor's orders.

"Well, where the hell is he?" you shouted, but it made no impression on her. This was New York, and Charles Olson was just one of suffering thousands who needed attention.

Finally, a doctor came in, a young intern. You introduced me to him as Dr. Boer, and then I left the room so that he could make an examination.

Outside in the hall, a gaunt, elderly lady, looking exhausted, was leaning against the wall, a bandage on her arm where I found out she had been given a shot to tranquilize her. Her husband, she told me, shared the room that you were now in, and he was being operated on for a blood clot in his leg. He had been in the operating room since early that afternoon and was still there. She had been waiting all this time for him, alone, in the dark of the hallway. I tried to cheer her up, but she was too honest with herself not to know how grim it all was. She nodded routinely at all gestures of sympathy.

Suddenly the intern came out into the hall and said to me, "Dr. Boer, I wonder if you would assist me with this patient. I don't seem to understand him."

I told him immediately of course that I was not an M.D. but a Ph.D. He reacted as if this meant I was a leper, his disappointed face crunching to a frown. But then he decided that perhaps I could help after all by interpreting you to him.

When we walked back into the room, you said, angrily, "Cholly, for Christ's sake, will you please tell this guy what's wrong with me. I told him it's all on my charts already anyway, but he keeps asking me the same old questions"

The intern explained that he had to do a preliminary examination, and that in all probability this hospital would have to repeat all the tests that were done at Manchester. Hospital policy.

You shrugged, and the intern began by asking you if you had ever had any problem with your ear.

"With my ear! For Christ's sake will you please read my record!"

The intern made a note on his clipboard. Then he asked if you had ever had any problems with your lungs.

At this you burst out laughing, turned to me, and said, "Did I ever, boy, wow! Cholly, remember that time in the Buffalo Hospital, ha, ha, when you, I, and who was it, Brover? yeah, ha, ha, went down to the lobby and . . ." and you went on to recall all the various times you had been in hospitals.

The intern took notes, and went on with other questions, but you replied to each with a joke, or a story, or even with a little discourse on metaphysics. The intern looked baffled and flustered. He didn't understand, or recognize, the complexity of this genius we had just brought in from the provinces.

I was still stinging a bit from our encounter in the hallway, but I could see that we were getting nowhere and that you were being difficult when you shouldn't have been. Nonetheless, I was on your side. I decided it was time to set the intern straight on a thing or two.

"I think I should point out to you, sir," I said, as formally as I could under the circumstances, "that Mr. Olson is a distinguished and brilliant American poet, and that the difficulty you're having in understanding him at first has been experienced by *millions* of his readers all over the world in twenty-eight languages when they too first encountered his voice. But I assure you that if you will only pay very close attention to what he is actually saying you will find him quite comprehensible and in fact quite interesting!"

I was more tired than angry but I felt I had to say it. You were sitting up in bed there beaming at me all through my little speech. Then, suddenly, you faked indignation and said, "What do you *mean* I'm difficult to understand! I'm the most articulate goddamn poet in this whole fucking country, Cholly Boer, and don't you ever forget it!"

"I know you are," I said, "but *he* doesn't," but the whole situation had become ridiculous by now and the intern very firmly suggested that I wait outside while he finished the examination without my professional assistance.

Your own interest in the theory of your cancer was extraordinary. You told the doctors that you thought it had all started in your throat. They said that was impossible. It could only start that way in women. At this you became very excited. "Follow that up!" you said, "because I *am* more woman than man. The woman is the creative part of me. All artists are part woman."

On another day, you said, "I've got it! It *is* the liver! I'm Prometheus, because Prometheus got it in the liver!"

The pain in your ear was still unbearable. None of the tests seemed conclusive as to where the source of the pain was. (The Manchester Hospital had its own theories, of course, but these were still to be proven by the New York Hospital.)

Then one day a delegation of doctors came in and said, "We find the pain you're getting is coming from a special nerve called 'the maximus nerve.'"

You looked at them and gasped.

One day I arrived at the hospital too early for visiting hours. I decided to pass the time having lunch. There was no cafeteria on the first floor, nothing but empty corridors of massive walls bearing, in large gold letters, the names of countless millionaire benefactors of the last half century—wall after wall of Vanderbilts and Whitneys, Rockefellers and Goulds, Guggenheims and Harrimans. The whole gang had been here apparently, hundreds of them. They met you as soon as you came down in the elevator from your own humble suffering scene into the expensive testimony of theirs. I was impressed. But it was all very dim. There seemed to be no artificial lighting in these halls, only the rare December daylight from an occasional window barely reflected in the gold of these great names.

I found my way, nonetheless, down into the depths of the place to the cafeteria. Nearly every seat at the several rows of counters was taken, but I found one in the corner and sat down to lunch. The waiters were quarreling among themselves about something.

A rather elegant woman, about your age, Charles, late fifties, came in. She couldn't find a seat. My coat was on the one next to me so I put it on my lap and indicated to her that there was a place. She thanked me very graciously and took off her fur coat which she put on the little swinging door that separated the customers' section from the waiters'.

Suddenly one of the waiters started yelling at her that that was no coat rack, lady, what do you think this is? She quickly got up and moved it, but was shaken. She was trembling. I gave her my menu, because the service was slow and it didn't appear that she would get one otherwise. She ordered tea, and thanked me again. We starting talking.

"Are you visiting someone?" she asked.

I told her all about you, Charles, how we had come down from Connecticut a few days earlier, what was wrong with you, what our hopes were.

"Well," she said, somewhat mechanically, as if it were a set speech she made every day, "they're very good here, and if anyone can help your friend, they can." She was still trembling.

She explained that she was "an auxiliary volunteer" who came once a week to help the staff, essentially by visiting people and keeping them busy. She was more interested, however, in the University of Connecticut, which she had never heard of.

"Is it one of those state schools?" she asked. "Do you have problems with riots there, too? What kind of students go there, poor ones? Are they industrious, or just troublemakers?"

I tried to explain to her that these were difficult times for students, for people generally, that there was a war on, that the pressures this society placed on people were sometimes staggering. But while she listened politely, it made no impression on her that there could even be reasons for such things.

"My husband has given each year to Princeton and Dartmouth," she said, in quavering tones, "but I think for the last time! People just aren't grateful anymore."

Suddenly she asked me if I had seen the latest Broadway play acclaimed by the critics, *Butterflies Are Free,* telling me what Walter Kerr had said of it. It was a truly inspiring play, she went on, about a blind young man who lives an effective life in spite of his handicap.

"You really should make an effort to see the play while you're in town," she said. "It's good to know there are still some young people in this country who don't make trouble."

When I told you about her later, Charles, you laughed, but it was good to talk to her. I had spent so much time these past few months talking to you alone that I had almost forgotten what it was like to listen to other people. Not every American spent his or her time contemplating "the Heavenly Heart of the Middle Kingdom."

Toward the end of my conversation with her, she asked me for your room number. She wanted to drop in on you for one of her charitable visits. I gave her your number, but told her you had a lot of visitors.

When I went upstairs to your room I was a little nervous. I didn't know whether you would be open to such an unusual visitor or explode at my presumption in giving her your room number. I thought she'd be fun for you. When was the last time, after all, that you talked to somebody who wasn't a poet or who didn't know someone else who was a poet? Nonetheless, I warned you that she might try to get you to see this inspiring new Broadway play while you were "in town."

"Well, by all means!" you said, laughing. "Bring 'em all on!"

Unfortunately, she never showed up.

On New Year's Eve Glenis Lobb went in to see you, bearing in hand your favorite dessert, coffee jello. You had told her once before that it was your favorite dessert but that you never got to eat it.

135

"Only wives can make coffee jello," you said, in that charming way you had of appealing to the wifely in women.

Glenis obliged by making a big bowl of it. And with the jello came pink chrysanthemums, which you immediately said were your favorite flowers.

"Capricorns make the best poets," you told her, thinking no doubt of your own birthday, which had just passed on December 27, "and Scorpios make the best wives." Glenis, however, was a Sagittarius.

You told her how you and your first wife, Connie, had lived in New York in the 1940s, and how much you had liked the city then. Connie would go out in the morning to a fruit store on 8th Street to get fresh fruit for a salad she would make you for breakfast. You loved to eat big salads of fresh fruit for breakfast. But you disliked the city now.

"It's past its peak," you said, "and it certainly hasn't improved any since then."

You would sit sometimes in the solarium on the twelfth floor, looking out at it all, pleasureless. The hospital, at East 68th Street, had an extraordinary view of ziggurat Manhattan, especially at night, the city's billion-dollar neon noise seeming a vast silent movie in the enforced peace of the solarium. How distant was Gloucester, I thought, where Maximus knew most men on the street by first name, knew each eighteenth-century house as few men know their own, knew each evening's shriek of hungry coastal birds as signal and hearkening to his own great appetite. Gloucester was another land, another time, and no man could be Maximus to New York.

One afternoon we were sitting in the solarium when a special messenger came up with a package for you from the Rizzoli Bookstore on Fifth Avenue. You tipped the man five dollars and opened it. It was a copy of your book, *The Distances,* in a new Italian translation, called *Le Lontananze.* This was the first copy out, and you were proud of it; proud too that your work was being translated into other languages. You gave it to me, since I knew Italian, and had me read some of it to you, wanting to hear for yourself whether the rhythms in Italian would sound the same as your own. You were pleased and satisfied that they did.

> Ciò che non cambia / è la volontà di cambiare
> What does not change / is the will to change

You kept telling the doctors now that you needed another ten years to finish your work.

"Ain't it a bitch," you said, "to die at 59! me, of all people!"

You would make jokes about it. You would treat your death, at least in front of other people, as some kind of routine occasion. And you were overwhelmed when friends came now to see you, friends from Black Mountain days, poets and writers flying in from Vancouver and Berkeley, from Buffalo and Gloucester and New York. Some would pretend that it would all pass over, that you would get well again. You would laugh at these, heartily, sympathetically, fondly. Others would be more realistic. You would laugh at them too. Someone even asked you if you had any particular kind of ceremony in mind for your funeral.

"Nah," you said. "Just have all my friends stand around and talk about me. That's what I want, a good old-fashioned Irish wake!"

At one point you said to me, "Well, Cholly my boy, it looks like it's over, doesn't it?"

I told you that you couldn't die yet—that there were still a lot of secrets that everyone would like to know.

"There are?" you asked. "What?"

I told you that I, for one, would like to know who was buried behind Lufkin's Diner in Gloucester, referring to a line in one of your poems where you ask, dramatically, "What's buried behind Lufkin's Diner?"

You laughed. "Who do you think is buried there?" you asked.

I told you I had no idea.

"Lufkin, you dope!"

And yet, as I was to learn much later, it is not Lufkin at all who is buried behind Lufkin's Diner. In fact, nobody is. You had had a dream in which two children were murdered and buried there. In the dream, you saw them as "lovekin." The joke was on me. Twice.

Nor did I know then that, in telling you there were "secrets" we still wanted to know, you would take it as seriously as you did. You started writing a long and final essay, called "The Secret of the Black Chrysanthemum." It is a remarkable summary of the experience of your life. You placed the manuscript in a sealed envelope, on the cover of which you wrote, "The 'Secret' notes written this day December 16th and to be only opened & by Chas. Boer if & when otherwise still to be retained as mine."

One day, the last day in fact that I talked to you, you told me you were "looking forward to the visions that, they say, come to a dying man."

You had been a patient in the New York Hospital for two weeks, moved there originally in the hope that a liver transplant would be possible. It was not. The cancer had spread with cruel rapidity to other parts of the body. There was nothing further that this hospital could do. In fact, you had already wasted away considerably, your body ravished by the disease. Your great size seemed diminished. You had lost at least half your weight.

With the announcement from the hospital that they could do nothing further to save you came an unexpected addendum: you would have to be moved to another hospital. The New York Hospital was only for treatment—its beds scarce and at a premium and only for those who had a chance. You would have to be moved to another hospital to die. Who knows how long, went the hospital's argument, the act of dying would be prolonged? With cancer patients it could be weeks, months even, months of untold horror not only for the patient himself, least of all for the patient, but for those around him as well—family, friends, not to mention nurses and the staff.

Fair enough. The New York Hospital, which had one of the finest staffs in the world for treatment of this particular disease, did not seem the most appropriate place anyway for the end of your life. The city had taken a huge toll of all our spirits. Everyone wanted to get out of there.

There is one problem, however, that hospitals fail to acknowledge when they notify you to move elsewhere. No hospital will admit a patient who is only coming in to die. Death, they will tell you, is not a hospital's business. Healing is a hospital's business. This became immediately clear after a few preliminary phone calls.

There are, of course, special hospitals for terminal cancer patients. A doctor from one of these in New York, however, warned us that if there were to be any visitors, any family involved, he would not recommend it. He told ghastly stories where even his nurses would faint at the daily spectre of dying cancerous humanity around them.

I left for Connecticut again, hoping to find a small hospital there, close enough to New York to expedite a quick transfer, and far enough from New York to see the sun shine. You had liked the Manchester Hospital. It was small and pleasant. It was much too far to move back to Manchester now, but perhaps a similar Connecticut hospital nearer to New York could be found.

I called Lee Kugler again, since she had been a nurse in the

Norwalk Hospital at one time. Though now retired, she might have some influence. Together, we must have made a few dozen phone calls that night around the state. She finally found a doctor in Greenwich Hospital who was willing to admit you as his "patient." He assured Lee that he couldn't save her friend, but he knew how trying the situation could be, and offered to help. There was one problem, however. You would have to go on a waiting list for a bed. Only Greenwich residents could be admitted without waiting for beds, and no exceptions were made except through the Hospital Board of Trustees. If we could reach someone on the Board of Trustees, this doctor said, the red tape could be cut and things would speed up.

More phone calls. I called your daughter, Kate, in New York, to tell her that Greenwich would accept you and that you were on a waiting list. She too felt the urgency of getting you out of New York. Calls were then made to various people who might themselves have influence with members of the Greenwich Hospital Board of Trustees. To die with dignity in America was the same as living with dignity in America: a matter of permissions, of hierarchy and influence. Calls through a friend to the Episcopal Bishop of Greenwich. Calls to a graduate student at the University of Rochester whose family in Greenwich lived next door to the former president of Greenwich Hospital. And calls to others, favors and privileges, the dismal world of personal "connections."

I called the Greenwich Hospital the next day to check if anything had happened. You were Number 22 on the waiting list. It appeared that you would be admitted that day, but they would phone me as soon as they knew for sure.

I sat by the phone in my living room all that day waiting for the call. But at five o'clock I had to call Kate again to tell her that we would have to wait until tomorrow for word.

The next day I called the Greenwich Hospital again. You were now Number 16 on the waiting list. I asked the doctor how many patients normally got admitted in one day, and he said it could be twenty or none at all. He said that the Board of Trustees had not been moved to open up a bed, and he asked me not to call so often. So much for personal connections.

The next morning, when I phoned the Greenwich Hospital again, you were Number 8 on the waiting list. It looked promising. I waited at the phone all that day, certain that this was it. But the call didn't come. I called Kate again, telling her how sorry I was that it had continued like this. But I was convinced that tomorrow for sure you would be moved.

On the fourth day, I called the hospital and found that you were only fourth on the waiting list. They said they would call me sometime that day. I waited. Then, late in the afternoon, the phone rang. It was Kate. She said that you had suddenly lapsed into a coma and the doctors expected the end shortly. You would not have to be moved after all.

I was exhausted from the tension of the past few weeks, and disgusted with the sense of helplessness one faces in confronting hospitals. I asked Paul Kugler to drive me to New York that evening. I was too tired to drive myself. It was snowing out when we started, a blizzard's worth, and the roads were bad beyond belief. Sometimes we couldn't even see as far as the next car ahead. We finally made it to New York, however, or at least as far as the Triborough Bridge. We got to the center of the bridge when suddenly the car stopped dead. The gas gauge on my Peugeot wasn't working and the tank was empty!

It seemed appropriate. A great poet was dying and calamities were surely coming as a result. Calamities were coming daily, in fact, and why should they not strike the car too? If all your books ended "with an image of the vehicular," then the end of your life meant a stop to all vehicles. Paul managed miraculously to coast downhill from the middle of the bridge. At the bottom, as if by an act of mercy from the unknown gods of Manhattan, there was a gas station.

It was eleven P.M. on January 8 when we got to the hospital. The floor was deserted and in darkness. The doors of all the patients' rooms were open, as if the hospital were empty. The patients were all asleep. I walked by your door but saw no one around so I left for the night.

When I arrived at the hospital the next day, Kate's mother, Connie, was there. The three of us sat in the solarium for a while, discussing the events of the past week. When, a little later, I went in to see you, you were considerably more wasted than I anticipated, even after a lapse of several days. You seemed extremely gaunt, all evidence of your size and stature now vanished. In a coma, you continued mumbling, softly, but nothing you said was at all comprehensible. We took turns that day sitting in the room with you sometimes, in case visitors would come by, and sitting in the solarium the rest of the time.

There seemed very little to talk about anymore. Charles Olson, whose gifts and grandeur with the American language we had all come to love, could no longer speak to us, and though death itself was still to come, the absence of your voice was making itself felt, and beginning to hurt. A poet's silence can be a terrible thing. More terrible, I see now, than a poet's voice. In the frenzy of the previous weeks, there was little time to contemplate what this absence would really mean to us. It was, to a certain extent, unthinkable. To have known you at all was to keep your voice, somewhere, in the back of one's head, forever present, forever going. To have heard you read your poetry, or any poetry, once, was to alter forever the way one would hear poetry again. Or the way one would hear many things. Simply to have talked with you, to have savored the richness of your speech, "the joy and wit of the world" as you called it—who would have dreamed there could be an end to it?

The death of a poet is the most enigmatic death of all. Kings and presidents, yes, old soldiers, yes, fathers and sons even, but poets? It was hard for me to believe, that awful afternoon as I sat in the solarium, that you could perish as easily as other men; that a man whose time is given over, with God only knows what agonies, to the life and very breath of the language, to what is therefore most human in human life, could not somehow beat life at its own terms; and death being only one of its terms, could not somehow beat death too.

At about nine o'clock that evening, I went into your room for the last time. You were still mumbling, incomprehensibly, in the coma. I said good night to Connie and Kate, and put on my overcoat. I turned to look at you a final time, and suddenly, though all of your other words continued to be as incomprehensible as before, I heard you say, with the fullest clarity and calm, the one sweet word, "wonderful." "Wonderful."

Three days later, in Gloucester, I remember the coastal sun bright and steady, setting off the deathless whiteness of that town. A light snow on the ground from the night before was just noticeable. Charles Olson was buried that morning in the Beechwood Cemetery in West Gloucester, a far walk from the sea, but close enough to a schoolyard so that the voices of schoolchildren playing could be heard in the air during the brief ceremony. "The live air," you called it. And hearing them at play, I couldn't help thinking, then

143

and all through that day, of the adventurous few among them who in a few years perhaps would come across the poems of this man we buried so near them now. They would hear wonders of their city then, and a truth of it they could not find otherwise, as they struggled to live in whatever was left of it. Because of you, Charles, they would hear, and know, who they are.